PRAISE FOR *FLOURISH*

"Grace has quickly become one of our dearest friends. She lights up every room with her smile and radiates with hope everywhere she goes. At the core of her heart is a humility that runs deep. She has chosen to embrace the ever-changing seasons of life with a pure heart—allowing her to see the purpose in each phase. We have watched her allow God to use her voice to become an incredible communicator and her message has already impacted so many lives. Through her new book, she is going to inspire you to flourish in all that God has planned for your life."

—**DeLynn & Dino Rizzo, Executive Directors,
Association of Related Churches**

"A must-read…Overflowing with wisdom, fresh perspective, and life-changing paradigm shifts…Will give you strength to live with passion and purpose through every season of life."

—**Steve Robinson, Pastor of Church of the King, Author,
and Founder of Hope Today TV and Radio**

"*Flourish* is a gift. Grace Klein has been blessed with an exceptional and unique ability of seeing every person who crosses her path and loving them exactly where they are. She, with uncommon candor and kindness, shares the story of her life in a way that is guaranteed to bless and minister deeply to many, and I am so excited for you to read this book and to see Grace's heart printed on every page."

—**Chad Fisher, Lead Pastor, Rock City Church**

"In her book, Grace has masterfully, and with great precision, tackled a topic that many shy away from, in order to bring hope and clarity in a world of ever-changing seasons. She brings out the reality that God really does have the capability to cause us to grow and *flourish* in each one of those seasons…This book will help so many people navigate through the different seasons of their lives so they will not simply exist, but *flourish*."

—**Shaun Nepstad, Author of *Don't Quit in the Dip*,
Lead Pastor of Fellowship Church**

"Grace's beautiful writing is an invitation, in the face of time, to be resilient, outrageously devoted to life in the hands of a gracious God... My hope is you will find courage in your own heart as you hold this book and be reminded of life's gentle prodding toward the One who develops us in every season."

—**Dianna Nepstad, Pastor, Fellowship Church, Antioch, California**

"Grace has put her cards of transparency on the table for us to see how to survive when we do not have the answers, and how to create momentum in each of the four seasons that develop a thriving harvest on the other side of difficult seasons of our lives. Even if you are not in a winter season right now, *Flourish* provides the tools necessary that will allow the reader to develop the muscle memory needed to succeed well beyond survival when those hard times come upon us."

—**George L Davis, Senior Pastor, Impact Church, Jacksonville, Florida**

"Grace Wabuke Klein has given us a beautiful look into the many trials and triumphs that accompany the different seasons in our lives as we journey with God...*Flourish* will not only be an inspiration to many but will also provide a roadmap that can be returned to again and again as we journey through our own seasons of life, learning to trust God in it all."

—**Mike and Barb Cameneti, Lead Pastors, Faith Family Church**

"We have had the privilege and joy of being Grace's pastors for over twenty years while she was on staff with us. We saw firsthand Grace's unwavering faith and tenacity as she navigated the hardest of times, all the while trusting God and not her circumstances. Grace is gut-wrenchingly candid about her journey about being single for several decades while Mr. Right was nowhere in sight. Grace never settled, but instead poured herself into living life to the fullest and walking in divine purpose. *Flourish* gives the reader powerful, practical insight, motivation, and tools to enter into a more intimate relationship with God."

—**Dr. Jim and Marguerite Reeve, Founding Pastors, Faith Church**

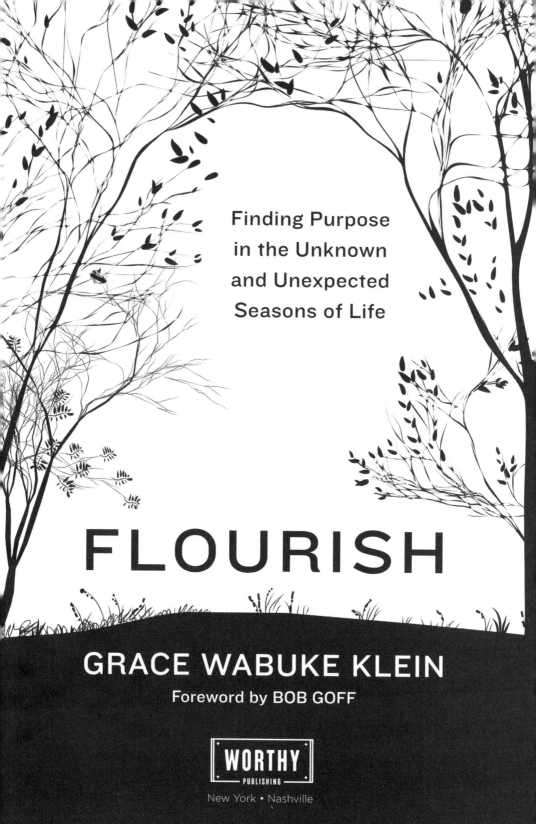

Finding Purpose
in the Unknown
and Unexpected
Seasons of Life

FLOURISH

GRACE WABUKE KLEIN

Foreword by BOB GOFF

WORTHY
PUBLISHING

New York • Nashville

Worthy
Hachette Book Group
1290 Avenue of the Americas, New York, NY 10104
worthypublishing.com
twitter.com/worthypub

First Edition: August 2023

Worthy is a division of Hachette Book Group, Inc. The Worthy name and logo are trademarks of Hachette Book Group, Inc.

The publisher is not responsible for websites (or their content) that are not owned by the publisher.

The Hachette Speakers Bureau provides a wide range of authors for speaking events. To find out more, go to hachettespeakersbureau.com or email HachetteSpeakers@hbgusa.com.

Worthy Books may be purchased in bulk for business, educational, or promotional use. For information, please contact your local bookseller or the Hachette Book Group Special Markets Department at special.markets@hbgusa.com.

Library of Congress Cataloging-in-Publication Data has been applied for.

Dad, there's not a day that went by in this writing process that I did not think about you and the wisdom you spoke into my life. So much of who I am is because of all you modeled and taught me. You made me want to know the God that you knew. Thank you for introducing me to the Lord as a young girl and encouraging me to become all He created me to be. Although you are now in heaven and not able to see the completion of this book, you are the one who supported me through all the seasons described in it. You were the consistent voice praying for me and pointing me to Jesus throughout the forty-four years we had together. Because of you, I have been able to walk in my purpose and truly flourish.

CONTENTS

CONTENTS

PART 4: SUMMER

FOREWORD

By Bob Goff

I'm so glad you picked up this book! I want to introduce you to my friend Grace. I have been telling people about her from the moment our paths crossed over five years ago. If you have not met Grace, the first thing you'll notice is her smile that lets you know you are loved. You will also experience her humility. She's got a voice that carries far in people's lives because she actually cares about people. Grace is also trustworthy. She doesn't say things just because they're the right things to say. She says things that are right. And it won't take long for you to see that Grace loves God. She has taught me more about loving and loving Jesus than any dozen other people.

I met Grace several years ago during the first Dream Big workshop I hosted in my hometown. She and about forty other eager dreamers had come to San Diego to lean into their dreams. The goal of my Dream Big course is to dive deeper into the ideas people have been floating around in their heads and start probing them to move forward. Grace came to the Dream Big workshop with big ambitions! She wanted to become a speaker so she could share what she had learned about love and acceptance and setbacks and Jesus. But there were some obstacles getting in her way. I knew she had something to say, and people needed to hear her voice. She didn't need more information about her ambition; she just needed an opportunity. She had never really had a shot at speaking in front of a large crowd. Without a big stage with loads of cameras, she didn't have a video showing her speaking to demonstrate that she had what it takes to get on other stages. It was a catch-22 that probably sounds familiar to anyone with a similar ambition.

When Grace and I met, I was scheduled to speak to three thousand people a few days later. I knew there would be plenty of high-end video cameras pointed at the stage, so I invited Grace to join me. I didn't clear the idea with anyone first. We just walked out onto the stage holding hands. I walked with her to the microphone, whispered "Go," and stepped out of the camera frame. I'll probably never get invited to speak there again, but you know what? Grace crushed it. It was the most inspiring talk I've heard in ages. I wasn't surprised when everybody loved her. Grace speaks all over the place now. She could have had 1,001 complaints about the setbacks and barriers both behind and in front of her. She could have played the comparison game and thought everyone else had it easier or was a better speaker than she was. Instead she walked her own path and it led her right to that microphone. She did her best and it was way more than enough.

I'm so glad Grace has put some of her thoughts on paper. *Flourish: Finding Purpose in the Unknown and Unexpected Seasons of Life* is how she has lived her life. We all go through setbacks and challenges that leave us discouraged or a little worn down. We should not be surprised when setbacks happen. It's part of being alive. Instead we need to lean into them. Always moving forward. It isn't fun, but it works. In this book, Grace draws insight from her winter season and shows us how to do that. Grace brings encouragement and perspective on how to walk through such seasons. She shows us that there is something valuable developing in us. She speaks difficult truths but she does it with her palms up. What she shares helps us see that there is a purpose in each season of our lives. The challenges we experience don't mean we should fold up our tent and go home. It means just the opposite.

We need to find purpose in these seasons. Grace is someone who has done that. In this book, she helps you take the next step in the season you are in. She is a proven guide on unknown and unexpected paths. Sometimes when we ask for answers, God sends us a friend. I'm thrilled to introduce you to my friend Grace. She is a trusted voice who will walk this journey with you, celebrating your victories and helping you through difficult times. I encourage you to listen to what she has to say. We both want to see you flourish!

FLOURISH

unearthed from my journals:

Today I woke up in a bad space. I woke up wondering if a man will ever pursue me. Will he see my inner and outer beauty? Will I ever have my own family?...God, this is not what I expected my life to look like at this point! Are the dreams in my heart ever going to happen?!...God, I'm falling into an unhealthy place. We're going through another season of baby showers and bridal showers at church. Lord, You have got to give me something, a life preserver, because I'm sinking fast. I don't know if I can make it through this season.

There Was
No Forecast for
This Season

I got out of my car, keys in one hand and takeout in the other, glad that the blinking light on the dashboard had not caused any issues on the drive home. After a quick stop to the mailbox, I headed inside the house, set everything down on the counter, and reached for the remote to turn on the TV. The familiar voice of the news anchor filled the silent living room and welcomed me to my otherwise lifeless home.

I thumbed through the mail as I headed toward the trash can. Mostly the usual...bills, ads, and more bills. The corner of an off-white envelope stuck out among the other envelopes and brightly colored ads. I flipped to it, intrigued to have possibly received some personal mail. I found the envelope and my heart sank. Miss Grace Wabuke. *Not another one.* I sighed heavily. The fancy calligraphy was a telltale sign of a wedding invitation. An obligatory event to celebrate a friend getting what *I* wanted more than anything. Another reminder of the fact that I was still single, and all my friends were getting married, having kids, and seeing their dreams come true, while I remained stuck.

I tried to remember who recently announced their engagement on social media. There had been so many proposals over the holidays, it could be a number of couples. I inadvertently rolled my eyes and let out another sigh as I thought about what this was going to mean. Having to muster up every ounce of energy to put a smile on my face and act like I was enjoying the festivities while my heart was breaking. I was not looking forward to attending showers and participating in a host of overplayed bridal-themed games that were fun during my twenties but irritating fifteen years later. Going through the emotions of oohing and aahing as gifts were unwrapped, while trying to hold back tears and wondering why it wasn't me who was getting married. Only to be followed by weeks of agonizing over who I was going to sit with at the wedding ceremony and reception. It would be so much easier if I were with my future spouse. *"Maybe you'll meet him at the wedding,"* my married friends would say, in an attempt to encourage me. *"God is preparing you,"* they'd add, not realizing their well-meaning words left me wondering how all the younger brides were somehow more "prepared" than I was.

God, why are You making me wait so long? Why can't You just bring my husband? You created the world in six days; surely this is not too difficult for You! I had cried out to God many times, but this time was different. This time, I was done. I was forty years old and done with being single. I was done with guys who were afraid of commitment and the ones who were intimidated by a woman in leadership. I was done with going on dates, only to look into eyes that glazed over the minute I told them I worked in full-time ministry. I felt so alone in my empty house. The disappointment, heartache, and anxiety suffocated me as I tried to sleep to escape my pain. It seemed like I had been in this winter season forever and my prayers continued to go unanswered. I wondered if anything was ever going to change. I could not understand God's purpose or direction in this unknown season. I was hurt and confused by how a loving God could see me in such pain and not do something about it. Well, I was done waiting for God. I did not see the point of enduring such agony and was ready to take things into my own hands.

Maybe you can relate. You've found yourself in a space where life does not look like you expected. You thought you would be living your best life by now, doing what you always dreamed. Maybe you thought you would be married and have a family by now. You didn't think it would be so hard to get pregnant, but with each monthly cycle, you face the disappointment of an unanswered prayer. Perhaps you had great plans to be your own boss with a thriving business. You didn't expect the grind of an entrepreneur to be so hard. You thought your ride-or-die friends would always have your back. You never expected them to turn on you and not celebrate your success. Maybe you did not expect your health to begin to fail, to have your marriage implode, or your kids lose their way…yet here you are. In the center of an unknown or unexpected season of life. Why would God allow you to enter such a painful place? Why won't He just speak, extend His hand, send angels, and do something—anything to change your circumstances? Even the unconventional ways He worked miracles would be welcome. Anything to shift the current situation.

I hear you, my friend! Waiting can be so frustrating. Whether you're waiting for marriage, to have a child, healing, financial resources, a business or an idea to take off, time can seem to stand still. Especially as we watch others get the very thing we have been praying to receive. We're used to instantly getting what we want. We google anything to get instant information. We click a few buttons and instantly transfer money. We place an order at a restaurant or put something in the microwave and get food within minutes. However, there is no "instant" button when it comes to the way life unfolds. The interrupted plans and idle dreams leave us questioning our way in the midst of an unknown path. We wonder which step to take next, which direction to head toward, and what to do with our life. We agonize over whether the dreams in our hearts will happen. I totally get it. My plan, which was carefully crafted in junior high school, was to get good grades so I could get into a prestigious university, graduate from college, establish my career, and be married and have a family by thirty. Well…thirty came and went and I was still single. So did thirty-five and forty! For the love! Clearly God and I were on different timelines! Arrggh! I kept asking the Lord why He was having me wait so long to see the answer to my heart's desire. Why was I having to endure years of waiting while a steady stream of younger girls walked straight from graduation, down the aisle, and to the altar. Perhaps you can relate to the loneliness, depression, heartache, or at the very least the frustration of life not turning out as you had planned. Watching people who are not even trying to get pregnant announce their surprise while you invest time, money, and all available resources into trying to see two solid lines on a plastic stick. You've taken prenatal vitamins and fertility drugs, you've invested in IUI, but while your friends are discussing baby names, you're having conversations with your spouse about surrogacy and adoption.

It can be so hard to trust and wait on God. With each passing season, it feels like time is fading and the stakes are getting higher. There's no snooze button on the biological clock. It just keeps getting louder and louder. There's no Band-Aid that can contain the gushing heartache and pain. The wound only gets deeper with each passing day. As the months go by, there's an increasing drive to make something happen. Especially during the holidays, when it seems like everyone else's life is so perfect and you are missing out. You see all the "December to Remember" Lexus promotions on TV, but there's no one in your driveway surprising you with a car. The syrupy diamond commercials air nonstop, but there's no "kisses beginning with Kay." The endless stream of Christmas cards with happy, smiling families amplifies the grief, numbness, disbelief, anger, sorrow, and loneliness after a miscarriage. You had started imagining your baby's future from the moment you knew you were pregnant. And now all you have are shattered dreams of cuddling a little one in your arms and having a family of your own. Maybe you recently found yourself single again after a divorce or the loss of a spouse. Nothing prepared you for that trial. And as you grieve or try to move forward after the loss, you're not quite sure where or how you fit in social gatherings. Each holiday magnifies the fact that life does not look like you expected. The stress, anxiety, and lack of sleep is taking its toll on your body. For some of you, your health issue is serious and you're wondering if you will overcome the illness that is plaguing your body. You're concerned how fast your body is changing and afraid of losing control. You've been trying to brush off the everyday things you are having trouble remembering. You didn't expect memory loss would start so soon, and each day the fear of the unknown season ahead grows.

It can be so hard to find our way and not lose heart in the midst of life's challenges. You have cried out for help, for someone who will listen, someone who will see you and let you know that you are not alone in this. Someone who will walk with you through the mess and help you breathe through the pain. Someone who gets that the struggle is real! My friend, I hear you! That's the reason I wrote this book. I know the frustration of trying to understand why an all-powerful God does not do something about the situation you're in. I know what it's like to be surrounded by people and yet feel so alone because no one understands what you're going through. I know the disappointment of things not looking like you thought they would, and the hopelessness that comes from not seeing any sign of change. You are trying to just keep it together and not lose your mind as you deal with your current situation. I want you to know that what you are facing is not the end of your story. This is not the final chapter. God has more for you. God has been working in your life. He is currently working. And He will continue to work in your life. He is still writing your story. You will breathe again. You will hope again.

I can say that because of what I have seen God do in my life and in the lives of so many others. He is faithful. He is faithful to heal you. He is faithful to help you. *And* He is faithful to hold you in times when your prayer is not answered as you expected. After years of waiting for God and trusting His timing, I finally experienced the fulfillment of His promises. He gave me so much more than my heart desired when He brought my husband, Phil, into my life. For over twenty years, I had been crying out to God and waiting for Him to answer my prayer. And after such a long winter season, He suddenly answered my heart's desire. Very quickly, Phil and I knew we had something special. We courted for some time, and eight months later, I finally walked down the aisle for the first time a week before my forty-third birthday. No, that is not a typo. I got married at forty-two. (More on that later!) Phil was not only my first boyfriend, he was my first kiss. Just to clarify, that's not because there weren't guys who had been interested in me—there were plenty of blind dates, speed dates, and "What was I thinking?" dates that I am desperately trying to forget. But I strongly believe God brings two people together for a purpose. He brings them together to do greater things for the Kingdom than they are doing on their own. I was doing some significant things, and I was determined to live my life as I waited for someone who was also doing great things. I just didn't think it would take that long! We've now been married five years, and in that time, I've experienced the reward of waiting on God's best.

It's easy to celebrate and walk with purpose when life is going as planned. When you've received your miracle and you're loving life. The sky's blue, flowers are blooming, and birds are chirping. Living life with purpose happens effortlessly during such idyllic times. If that's where you're at, I'm celebrating with you in this summer season!

But chances are, that's not what things look like right now. It's not why you picked up this book or why a friend recommended it to you. Your world looks more like winter. The clouds are gray and overcast, the ground is bare, and the only birds present are vultures circling above in the sky. It's as if they recognize the discouragement, anxiety, loneliness, resentment, and frustration you are feeling. They pick up the scent of hopelessness that comes after praying for healing and not seeing any change but instead things just getting worse. They sense your heartache from not having a family of your own and the sting you feel when friends complain about their kids or take the gift of parenthood for granted. The worry and anxiety consuming you because of the destructive choices your son or daughter is making. A spouse who is distant or unfaithful and no longer wants to fight for your marriage. You never expected to find yourself single again at this stage in life. Maybe it's the financial stress of having debt collectors call as you try to figure out how you are going to pay the bills and put food on the table. The heartache of a dream that is delayed. The frustration of praying, fasting, and crying out to God and seeing nothing happen. Nothing except for friends getting answers to *their* prayers and seeing *their* dreams come true. I know what it's like to no longer want to pray, no longer want to believe, no longer want to trust God, because you just can't take the hurt of having your hopes shattered again.

If you can relate at any level, I want you to know I wrote this book specifically for you. While I wish I could make that prayer, that desire, that longing in your heart happen, only God can do that. I can, however, be a trusted friend in the midst of the struggle. A friend who will stand and believe with you in the waiting. A safe place to vent and a shoulder to cry on with the freedom to have raw conversations. And most important, a friend who will call you out in order to keep you from doing something crazy you will later regret. No matter what you are facing, you do not need to go through it alone. If you'll allow me, I want to journey through this season with you because it can be disheartening to trudge through it yourself. (I've tried that and it didn't go well.) I want to offer words of encouragement and perspective from having walked (and at times crawled) on a similar road. Now that I'm on the other side, I can say from personal experience that God is faithful. He hears your prayers and knows your heart's desires. Even though it may not look like it, God is still working. He has always, is currently, and will continue to work in your life. Even when it seems like nothing is happening and nothing is changing in the situation, God is still at work. We have but to open our hearts and minds to see what cannot be seen with our natural eyes. It is my goal along this journey for you to recognize the hand of God in your life and embrace what He is doing in the process.

I believe it's not chance or accident that you have this book in your hands. What you hold represents over twenty years of walking through an unknown and unexpected winter season. The priceless wisdom gained, the hard lessons learned, and everything in between. I share transparently about my mistakes with the hope you can avoid similar pitfalls. As the chapters unfold, my hope is you will also begin to find purpose in your current season. I have prayed that the words on each page will bring you hope. That the practical applications will provide tools to help you fight the battles of discouragement, disillusionment, and depression. And that the stories will be God's way of encouraging you of His faithfulness.

Throughout this book, I want to be a friend helping you stand in the midst of your struggles and encouraging you to walk by faith through the seasons of life. To be someone you can lean on when it hurts too much to keep moving forward. A friend who will cry with you in the lonely, hard times and also celebrate your answered prayers, accomplishments, and milestones with you. Who will walk with you through the seasons of life.

Just as nature graciously transitions from one season to the next, I want you to live and find purpose in the fall, winter, spring, and summer seasons of life. Some seasons are more enjoyable than others. Some make you wish you had a remote control that could fast-forward a few months to the next season. Unfortunately, unlike nature, in which there is a specific time frame for each season, life does not have such parameters. Life's seasons can last several months, years, or even decades. But I believe you can flourish in whatever season you're currently in. You can live your life and walk in your purpose. Psalm 92:12–13 promises, "The righteous will flourish like a palm tree, they will grow like a cedar of Lebanon; planted in the house of the Lord, they will flourish in the courts of our God" (NIV). As we embark on this journey, you will begin to establish roots that go deep and help you stay planted and withstand life's storms. You will discover purpose in each season:

- Fall is a time of shorter days, cooler temperatures, and brightly colored leaves cascading to the ground. Trees intentionally release their leaves in preparation for the winter season. In the fall season of this book, we will work through releasing things in our lives. Letting go of unhealthy relationships, offenses, hurts, bad habits, toxic friendships, pride, comparison, unforgiveness, and all types of other issues. We will learn the purpose of letting go, how to release offenses, and to make room for the new things that come in the spring.
- Winter is a time when things are dormant, and the nights are

long and cold. In life, winter is a season of isolation, anxiety, disappointment, depression, heartache, pain, unanswered prayers, unexpected challenges, and unknown futures. This section will provide hope and insight on how to stand and keep the faith through the winter season. You will discover that some of the greatest lessons of life are often learned in and through life's storms, which shape us and make us stronger.

- Spring is a time of warmer weather, melting snow, and signs of new life. Flowers start to bloom, and trees begin to bud. God delights in doing new things and He takes great pleasure in having us be part of them. Isaiah 43:19 says, "Behold, I am doing a new thing!" (ESV). Rarely do His plans make sense to our finite minds. We prefer to stay in our caves where things seem safe. But God has so much more for us. Flowers and trees do not bloom in caves, and we cannot flourish in them either. We need to be open to stepping out into the unknown and uncomfortable. It is here that God does His best work. Just as a seed relies on the sun, water, and good soil to grow, we need to rely on God, His Word, and opportunities He brings to help us grow. As we walk through the spring section of this book, you will see the value of opening up to new experiences, people, ideas, and perspectives.

- Summer is the warmest season of the year, with bright, sunny days, flowers blooming, and trees providing fruit. The days are long, birds are singing, and everything is flourishing. In this summer section, we will reflect on how the fall, winter, and spring seasons cultivated a level of faith and developed spiritual muscles within us. We will celebrate the character development, growth, and transformation that have taken place through the journey.

Full disclosure before we begin: This writing process has been one of the *hardest* things I have ever done. The fact that I actually finished writing the book is nothing short of a miracle. I had many "conversations" with the Lord about this assignment, giving Him more reasons than Moses did as to why I was not qualified to do what He was calling me to do. I argued that it would be more effective to give this project to any one of my friends who have written *New York Times* bestselling books. *If You really want to impact people*, I reasoned with the Lord, *it makes more sense to have those established authors write the content so it can reach the millions of people they influence around the world!* And just when I thought I had made my case, I would run into some of you at churches across the country, or y'all came up after a speaking engagement, and many more of you sent messages to me on social media, all asking the same questions: "Do you have a book, a blog, or any resources? I want to hear more about how you waited for God and did not compromise. How did you keep trusting in Him and not give up or lose hope?"

So I had to write what I learned and what I wished someone had shared with me in my darkest days. I had to tell you that you are not alone. You are not forgotten. There is more to your life's journey. You have a story to tell that will come from this winter season you are in. Someday, you will be able to help others who are in a similar situation because you will truly get what they are going through. There is a purpose on the other side of your pain.

Another thing to note: Revelation 12:11 says, "They overcame him by the blood of the Lamb and by the word of their testimony" (NKJV). Having been on this faith journey for over forty years, I have a number of testimonies and piles of journals with the tests and trials leading up to them. I always tell my friends and family, *If anything happens to me, take whatever you want, but find my journals and burn them.*

For the sake of us all, burn the journals! They are filled with tearstained pages from years of crying out to the Lord. The twenty-something who thought she had life all figured out. The thirty-something who was shocked, hurt, and frustrated that life wasn't going as planned. And the forty-something who very unsuccessfully tried to take things into her own hands and help God speed up the process—'cause He clearly needed my skills in making things happen! I've included sections from those journals in this book to encourage you that, no matter where you are at, God sees you, He has not forgotten you, and He hears the cry of your heart. While we may not understand it at the time, He is working on our behalf. If He can take this hot mess of a type A overachiever and get her to give up trying to make things happen and surrender, He can do anything.

And guess what? His plans are so much better than anything I had imagined for myself. Isn't that always the case? So whether you're lazily enjoying your favorite latte at a coffee shop, or at home curled up on your couch with a box of tissues and chocolates, I would love to join you on your journey. To pull up a chair and hear what you are going through, and if you would allow me, to share a few stories from my journey to encourage and let you know that you are not alone and you will make it through this.

I'm excited to start this journey with you and can't wait to see what the Lord reveals to you along the way. I'm honored you would allow me to be part of the process—not as an expert, but simply as one who has been down a similar path and learned a few things along the way. While I may not have the most eloquently crafted words, what I do have is story after story of God's faithfulness. And if you stick with me to the end, together we will celebrate the fruition of standing and keeping the faith through the seasons of life. You will experience the deeper intimacy you have been longing for as you grow in your faith and get to know Him in a deeper way. You will experience freedom as you release lies, past hurts, and things that are keeping you stuck. You will be empowered as you discover your identity, authority, spiritual DNA, and heritage. You will learn how to stand in the winter season and develop unwavering spiritual roots through the unseen, "underground" disciplines of prayer, worship, and absorbing the Word of God. You will experience peace as you embrace that God is doing something in your life that can only come to fruition through the winter season. That He is with you in the waiting, the challenges, the heartache, the disappointments, and the storms of life. In the spring, you will be encouraged as you receive the new thing God is doing, and you begin to see the results of waiting and trusting in the Lord. As you look to Him, you will find purpose in the unknown and unexpected seasons of life. By the end of this book, we will be celebrating the unseen gifts that have been cultivated throughout each season. We will reflect on how we have drawn closer to God through the process and been transformed to be more like Him. I'm honored to walk with you through this journey. I pray some of the stories from my experiences will encourage you along the way. I pray Psalm 115: 14–15 over you: "May the LORD cause you to flourish, both you and your children. May you be blessed by the LORD, the Maker of heaven and earth" (NIV). Amen!

PART I

FALL

unearthed from my journals:

9/3/05

I am completely broken. Absolutely stunned!!! I thought he was the one I prayed for and now I find out he's seeing someone else! I feel like my heart has been ripped out, ripped apart, and trampled on. This is the exact opposite of what I was believing for. It seems like every area in my life is at a standstill. My heart hurts so bad.

5/5/10

When will this crazy cycle ever stop?! I feel like I'm a hamster on a wheel running around but not going anywhere. My life does not look like how I thought it would. If I'm not going to be doing anything worthwhile, You might as well take me to heaven and rid me of this agony.

5/10/13

Found out Sarah [name changed] just had another baby! While I'm happy for her, it absolutely devastated me! I still remember when she came to UC Berkeley during my junior year and how I supported her through all she went through in her first year of college. Now she is married with 2 kids and has her doctorate. I can't bear to go on Facebook anymore with everyone posting pictures with their spouse and kids. It's a constant eyesore, an arrow through my heart, a continual reminder of what I do not have. My heart breaks to know I have fibroids growing in my uterus. Instead of experiencing the joy of having a fetus grow and develop inside me, I am experiencing nausea, pain, and weight gain from numerous growing fibroids. It would be one thing if I was 28, but now at 38, this is beyond discouraging. It is definitely not what I pictured my life would look like.

5/18/13

Lord, it's been such a painful week. I am too hurt and drained to even talk about it. Actually, I do not even want their names to grace my journal. As much as I was attacked regarding _____, You still told me to love. That is sooo painful, Lord. I pray You show me how to love in this situation, so I will be more like You, pass the test, and move forward.

CHAPTER I

Let Go and Live

"**M**r. and Mrs. Wabuke, I came over tonight to share something with you. You've been attending our church for a little while now, and um, I'm sure you may know that your presence has made some people uncomfortable. And I, um, can't have people coming to church and feeling uncomfortable. So I'm here to say that we, um, prefer that you, ahem, no longer attend our church."

The middle-aged man was perched at the edge of his chair in our living room, looking at the floor and then at my parents as he spoke. They sat across from him, dumbfounded. He shifted in the chair and cleared his throat as he wrung his hands together.

"You have to understand this is very difficult for me..." His words continued, but neither of my parents heard the rest of what he was saying. Dad reached for Mom's hand and gently squeezed it, partly to let her know he was there, but also to reassure himself this was not a bad dream. The whole thing seemed so surreal. The man from the local church stammered through the rest of what he had come to say as they sat in stunned silence.

We had been in Duluth, Minnesota, for only a few months. Having come from Uganda so my father could do graduate work at the

University of Minnesota, we had a lot to get accustomed to. As the only black family in the surrounding area, we stood out in our predominantly white neighborhood. While we were accepted by some, there were others who boldly told us to leave. In the midst of the subzero temperatures, we had our car tires slashed and a brick thrown through our living room window. People passionately told us to go back to where we came from. My parents sought community in the local church, as they thought they would surely be accepted there. They were surprised to find the welcome from the parishioners was colder than the snow and ice outside. The whispers, stares, and avoidance were in stark contrast to the smiles, hugs, and loving community we had received in our home church in Uganda.

The mounting tension made it difficult to breathe. Dad and Mom glanced at each other with eyes that communicated more than any words could in the moment. Peering across the room, they made sure I was still sleeping, before turning their attention back to the man who sat across from them. What he was saying was difficult to listen to, but what made it even harder was *who* was saying it to them. He wasn't an elder, a deacon, a trustee, or a church board member—not that they would have made it any more appropriate. It was the pastor of the church! His words pierced straight through to their hearts, creating a deep wound that no surgery or sermon message could heal.

How can this man call himself a pastor? Mom thought to herself as he continued speaking. *He's the one who should be fighting for us to stay, teaching the people it's wrong to make someone leave because they're different.* Her jaw clenched as he began suggesting other churches they could try. *How dare he have the audacity to come into our home, kick us out of the church, and tell us where to go?* She fumed inside.

Dad's head was pounding as he tried to decide what to do. This man was supposed to be their pastor, someone who prayed for them and taught them about Jesus. *How could he say this? A colleague at the*

University had suggested the church. And now the pastor is asking us to leave! How do you tell someone in spiritual authority who you barely know that they are way out of line? The tension in the air was overwhelming as the pastor concluded what he had come to say. In the uncomfortable silence, he shifted in his chair. Glancing up at the clock on the wall, he caught Mom's steely glare and quickly averted his gaze.

"I should be going now," he said as he cleared his throat and stood up.

Dad rose with him, but Mom remained fixed on the sofa. She crossed her arms and bit her lip; her brow furrowed and her eyes formed two slits. She knew if she got up, she would most likely say a few insolent words to the pastor and slam the door shut. Dad walked over and opened the front door to let him out. Their eyes met for a brief moment, and the pastor muttered what sounded like a farewell before he quickly darted from the house. Dad slowly closed the door and went back to where Mom was on the sofa.

He sat down next to her, uncertain what to say. They looked at each other in disbelief. It felt as if they were sharing the same bad dream. After several moments, Mom asked, "How could he say that to us?"

Dad silently shook his head, not able to formulate any words.

"How can they call themselves Christians?" Mom demanded. "How can they kick us out of their church? How can they worship a God of love and in the same breath tell us we are not welcome?"

Her questions hung in the air and expressed what they were both thinking. Dad's mind was racing with questions of his own. *Did we not hear God correctly? Wasn't it His plan for us to come to America? How can we raise our daughter in this country? What's going to happen when she goes to school?*

"What are we going to do now?" Mom's voice pulled Dad out of his thoughts. He reached over and wrapped his arms around her as tears rolled down her cheeks.

"I don't know," he whispered, shaking his head. "I don't know."

I was too young to understand all that took place in the conversation, and it wasn't until years later that my parents shared the specific details with me. But somehow, they made the remarkable decision not to let one man's words and lack of leadership or a church's reprehensible decision taint their view of God and His Church. As difficult as it was, they made the choice to forgive and let go. They made the decision to embrace God's life-giving words instead of the words of man. I'm so grateful they did not walk away from God or the Church because of that conversation. Our lives would have taken a very bitter and troubling path. Instead, they chose to model forgiveness and teach my siblings and me about God's love for us and all people. Thankfully, we eventually did find a church that welcomed us. We were able to make friends, worship God freely, and get involved in our new community.

⁂

Shorter days and cooler temperatures announce the arrival of fall. Nature's splendor comes into full display as the green foliage turns beautiful shades of red, orange, yellow, and brown. Soon the brightly colored leaves begin cascading to the ground as trees release them in preparation for winter. Fall represents a season of letting go. Releasing things in our lives that we have been holding on to for too long. Things that have kept us stuck and others that have prevented us from flourishing. Fall involves letting go of past hurts and offenses, unhealthy relationships, pride, comparison, unforgiveness, and all types of other heart issues.

But what if we are not ready to let go? Maybe the pain of uncovering an old wound is too great. The fear of the unknown is overwhelming. Or perhaps it's the discomfort of letting go of the familiar. It's so much easier to stick with what we've become accustomed to. But as our time together will reveal, holding on to those leaves can actually hurt you and cause you to wither and die. You need to let go in order to survive the winter. You need to let go in order to be ready for all that spring brings. You need to let go so that the past does not rob you of your future. You need to let go in order to live.

The process of letting go is not only part of the natural order of things; it's vital for life. We can see this in the life cycle of trees. There's a misconception that wind blows leaves off trees. The reality is that wind completes a very intentional process that started long before the billowy gust arrived. God designed nature that way. Leaves fall off deciduous trees so the tree can survive the winter. If the leaves were to remain on the tree through the winter, the tree would die. Did you know that? You can Google it, but to save you the time, let me give you the CliffsNotes version of what I discovered from doing a deep dive into the subject. During warm days, leaves make food through photosynthesis. They convert carbon dioxide and water into sugars, using the sun's energy. But if trees did not let go of their leaves in the autumn, when temperatures drop, the water in the leaves' veins would freeze, and the leaves would die. The tree would then be left with only dead leaves, no longer able to produce food, and thus the tree would eventually die.

So how does this process of intentionally releasing leaves happen? Well, there's a little-known fact that trees have hormones. The trees' hormones play an important part in the process of shedding their leaves. As days grow shorter and colder, a hormone is triggered that sends a chemical message to every leaf, essentially saying, "Time to go!" Once the message is received, cells called "abscission" cells appear at the place where the leaf stem meets the branch. Abscission is the shedding or natural detachment of parts of a plant or organism. Within a few days or weeks, every leaf on deciduous trees develops a thin, bumpy line of cells that push the leaf, bit by bit, away from the stem. When a breeze comes along, it basically finishes the process of something that started long before. Because the tree releases its leaves, the tree survives the winter, and there's room for new growth in the spring.

There is a lot of wisdom we can learn from that process. In life, certain things we hold on to can actually end up hurting us. It could be an unhealthy relationship, a negative way of thinking, or something from the past that is still controlling your life today. Letting go is not easy or pleasant, but we need to embrace the process in order to live. Perhaps you were the recipient of destructive words from a parent or adult who told you what happened was your fault, you were a mistake, or you would never amount to anything. Maybe it was from your spouse, whom you thought you would be with forever, suddenly telling you they wanted a divorce. Maybe it's not what was said to you, but what was said *about* you in other rooms and private conversations. The colleague who spread lies and turned the team against you. Your "friend" who used what they knew about you against you. Unfortunately, if you live your life for any amount of time, you will encounter haters and traitors. The hurt and betrayal we feel in the wake of their words is very real. No one should have to go through what they put you through. The problem comes when time has passed and we are still rehearsing and holding on to what they said and did to us. They have moved on with their lives and can barely recall the details of what happened, but you have painfully replayed it from multiple angles in high definition. Nothing flourishes in such a mental space. And while it may seem like you are getting to "have your say" in your head, that is not your purpose in life. You were created for so much more than that.

Jeremiah 17:7–8 puts it this way: "But blessed is the one who trusts in the LORD, whose confidence is in him. They will be like a tree planted by the water that sends out its roots by the stream. It does not fear when heat comes; its leaves are always green. It has no worries in a year of drought and never fails to bear fruit" (NIV).

The second half of this verse describes what it looks like to flourish. To live, operate, and be productive in a space free of fear and worry. That in the middle of life's challenges, trials, and struggles, you are able to be at peace and experience joy. And in the midst of the unknown and unexpected, when everyone else is freaking out about what the future holds, you can confidently walk with purpose. Who wouldn't want *that* in the world we are living in? Who wouldn't want to be fully present in each moment because they are not worried about the future, thinking of the many issues of today, or obsessed about what happened in the past?

So how do you experience that? The first half of the verse gives us some insight. The assurance of what we just read applies to those who trust in the Lord and place their confidence in Him. That is the key to flourishing. When we place our trust and confidence in ourselves or other people, that's when we begin to wither. Human beings were not created to sustain that. Only God can. To put that expectation on ourselves or someone else is setting things up for failure. It might appear to work for a short while, but just like building a house on quicksand instead of solid ground, pretty soon the foundation is going to crumble. God alone is the one that we can put our trust and confidence in.

One other vital point from this passage is that where you are planted matters. Verse 8 says, "They will be like a tree planted by the water that sends out its roots by the stream" (NIV). Note that it does not say it is planted or establishing roots by the swamp. That's because there is nothing in the murky water to sustain life. The flourishing tree is planted by living water that its roots can draw from. As we will expand on in future chapters, roots are vital for a tree's development, growth, and survival. They absorb the water and nutrients the trees need to live. So where roots extend to directly impacts the life of the tree. In the same way, the roots we do or do not develop impact our lives. Part of what we are going to focus on in our time together is developing roots. The kinds of roots that can withstand the storms of time, roots that go through the fire and do not smell like smoke, roots that survive through life's droughts and extended waiting periods. Those kinds of roots enable you to truly flourish. Those kind of roots do not just form in any soil. The seeds need to be planted and nurtured with intention.

Before we move on, it's important to take a moment and look at what the text says prior to the promise we just discussed. Jeremiah 17:5–6 shows us what happens when we do not trust in the Lord and place our confidence in him. "This is what the LORD says: 'Cursed are those who put their trust in mere humans, who rely on human strength and turn their hearts away from the LORD. They are like stunted shrubs in the desert, with no hope for the future. They will live in the barren wilderness, in an uninhabited salty land" (NLT). When we go through unexpected seasons in life and we don't know what to do, or how we will make it through, we have a choice of who we are going to turn to. God wants us to come to Him first. The books of the Bible read like a love letter from the Lord saying:

Come to Me. I have everything you need. Trying to hold on and do everything using your own strength or that of others is going to cause you to wither. You are not meant to carry all that weight. It pains Me to see you striving so hard on your own and trying to rely on others who were not designed to bear the load. Your misplaced trust is increasing your stress, worry, and anxiety. Turn your heart to Me. I created you, and I know you better than you know yourself. You can trust Me with that issue, that concern, that hurt, that offense. Let Me give you My peace as you let go of what you are carrying. Release it to Me so that you can flourish.

One of the things I love about trees is that they are an excellent example of what it looks like to "trust in the Lord" and place our "confidence in Him." Trees remain planted where they are and trust that they will have all they need. You do not see trees uprooting themselves and walking to a different location to try and get more food, shelter, visibility, access, or a more conducive environment. They trust that as they are doing what they were created to do, establishing their roots and reaching toward the Light, the God who made them will provide for their needs. As humans, we often lean toward self-reliance and admire people who are independent. However, trees show us that you truly flourish only when you are God-dependent. Trees know they cannot generate the sun, water, soil, and nutrients they need to survive. They need to rely on the Creator to provide. In the same way, we want to live our lives God-dependent, trusting in Him and placing our confidence in Him.

When you are having a difficult day or going through a challenging season in your life, I want you to take a moment and look at the trees outside your window, at a local park or wildlife preserve. Most of the trees have been there for decades, or even centuries. Through the seasons of heat, drought, wind, and storms, they are still standing. In months with leaves and months without, they are not wavering. As you look at the trees, I pray that you experience a sense of peace. That you will have an assuredness that just as God provided for them and protected them, He is able to do the same for you. That you will grow deep roots in your trust and confidence in Him.

One of the ways we develop deep roots is by making the decision to forgive ourselves and others. The Greek term for "forgiveness" (*aphiemi*) comes from a word that means "to let go." Just as trees are intentional in the process of releasing their leaves, we also need to be intentional in letting go of offenses, guilt, and shame. The choices we make regarding whether or not to forgive and let go not only affect us, they affect our children and potentially even future generations. I imagine most of us would agree that we'd rather do the work, although painful, to leave a legacy of love, grace, and forgiveness rather than bitterness, resentment, and unforgiveness. The purpose of this chapter is to continue the journey of finding purpose in the unknown and unexpected seasons of life. Forgiveness and letting go of anger, hurt, and past offenses is part of the process. I know we are starting deep, and there is some work to do; but I assure you, it is necessary and absolutely worth it. Just like a surgeon may need to remove something inside you in order for your health to improve, we need to do some heart surgery to prepare for what God has for you. But where and how does one start?* Sometimes before jumping into a process, it helps to hear from others who have gone through similar experiences and have been able to forgive and let go. I've found hope, encouragement, and strength to take the first steps as I've listened to and read stories of others who have walked a similar road and somehow been able to turn the corner. Over the years, I've read numerous stories of people who forgave unbelievable acts of betrayal, abuse, and injustice, and they have inspired me to take steps in my own journey of forgiveness. As we begin this process, I would love to introduce you to a few of these remarkable women who have pioneered a path for us.

Their names are Sojourner, Corrie, Elisabeth, and Jarena. Names not on any top influencers list. Not on any of *Forbes*'s lists. But if heaven were to generate a list of remarkable acts of forgiveness and

---

* There have been so many helpful books and resources written on forgiveness. As it is not the sole topic of this book, I encourage you to supplement this chapter with additional resources or professional counseling sessions.

love, I believe these would be some of the first names you would see. Of course, they would not view themselves as deserving of that. They would speak of their deep conviction of how they were the first to need forgiveness and have received it from Jesus. And if they could speak to you regarding releasing matters of the heart, I believe each of them would have something so profound for us to learn from their stories and experiences. You see, it's one thing to learn forgiveness from a book or the internet and another from someone who has lived it. From just these four women, we see the forgiveness of betrayal, discrimination, physical abuse, sexual abuse, imprisonment, child slavery, and murder.

Jarena Lee was born at a time when slavery was legal, and women could not own property or vote. It was long before electricity or running water. Although her family was free at the time of her birth in 1783, by the age of seven Jarena was separated from her parents to work as a live-in servant in a white household sixty miles away. She was later introduced to Christianity as a young adult and baptized in 1807 at the age of twenty-four. Not long after, she felt called to minister, but was denied the opportunity to preach by the bishop of the African Methodist Episcopal (AME) Church because of her gender. She married Joseph Lee in 1811, and seven years later, both her husband and their fifteen-month-old son died. Jarena continued to pursue her calling and was eventually publicly affirmed, making her the first African-American woman to preach the gospel publicly. Despite having little education and encountering consistent hostility, her ministry grew and experienced success. Over the course of twenty years, Jarena preached to black and white audiences in Maryland, Ohio, Pennsylvania, New York, New Jersey, and Canada. While the details surrounding her passing are not clear, what is etched in history is her legacy as the first African-American female preacher in the United States.

Corrie ten Boom was fifty-one years old when she, her siblings, and her father were arrested by Nazis for hiding Jews in their home during the Holocaust. Corrie and her sister Betsie were taken to Ravensbrück concentration camp, where they endured starvation, harsh labor, abuse, medical experimentation, and disease, resulting in Betsie's death. Corrie was released on December 31, 1944, one week before all the women in her age group were sent to the gas chambers. Corrie was later told that her release was due to a clerical error. Inspired by her late sister's example of love amid persecution, Corrie dedicated the rest of her life to traveling the world preaching about God's forgiveness and the need for reconciliation. One ministry engagement in 1947 was particularly memorable. She had just finished speaking at a church in Munich when a man walked forward to speak to her. She immediately recognized him:

[He was] the former S.S. man who had stood guard at the shower room door in the processing center at Ravensbruck. He was the first of our actual jailers that I had seen since that time. And suddenly it was all there—the roomful of mocking men, the heaps of clothing, Betsie's pain-blanched face. He came up to me as the church was emptying, beaming and bowing. "How grateful I am for your message, Fraulein," he said. "To think that, as you say, He has washed my sins away!" His hand was thrust out to shake mine. And I, who had preached so often to the people in Bloemendaal the need to forgive, kept my hand at my side.

Even as the angry, vengeful thoughts boiled through me, I saw the sin of them. Jesus Christ had died for this man; was I going to ask for more? Lord Jesus, I prayed, forgive me and help me to forgive him. I tried to smile, I struggled to raise my hand. I could not. I felt nothing, not the slightest spark of warmth or charity. And so again I breathed a silent prayer. Jesus, I prayed, I cannot forgive him. Give me Your forgiveness.

As I took his hand the most incredible thing happened. From my shoulder along my arm and through my hand a current seemed to pass from me to him, while into my heart sprang a love for this stranger that almost overwhelmed me. "I forgive you, brother!" I cried. "With all my heart!"

For a long moment we grasped each other's hands, the former guard and the former prisoner. I had never known God's love so intensely as I did then. And so I discovered that it is not on our forgiveness any more than on our goodness that the world's healing hinges, but on His. When He tells us to love our enemies, He gives, along with the command, the love itself.*

About a century prior to Corrie encountering the prison guard and facing her biggest challenge to forgive, another woman was delivering a historic speech challenging racial and gender inequality. "Ain't I a Woman?" was delivered by Sojourner Truth at a women's rights conference in 1851. Sojourner overcame incredible hardship and became a minister and trailblazer in the fight for abolition and for civil and women's rights. Born into slavery in New York in 1797, Sojourner was sold multiple times, beaten, and raped repeatedly. One of her five children was illegally sold when he was five years old. The heartache and anguish she and so many others endured are evident in the words to an original song she wrote:

---

* Corrie ten Boom, with Jamie Buckingham, *Tramp for the Lord* (London: Hodder & Stoughton, 1975), pp. 217–18.

I am pleading for my people—
a poor downtrodden race
Who dwell in freedom's boasted land
With no abiding place

I am pleading that my people
May have their rights [restored],
For they have long been toiling,
And yet had no reward.

They are forced the crops to culture,
But not for them they yield,
Although both late and early,
They labor in the field.

Whilst I bear upon my body,
the scores of many a gash,
I'm pleading for my people
Who groan beneath the lash.

I am pleading for the mothers
Who gaze in wild despair
Upon the hated auction-block,
And see their children there.

I feel for those in bondage—
Well may I feel for them.
I know how fiendish hearts can be
That sell their fellow-men.

Yet those oppressors steeped in guilt—
I still would have them live;
For I have learned of Jesus,
To suffer and forgive!*

In the midst of such injustice and abuse, Sojourner sang about forgiveness. While others in similar circumstances would be plotting revenge or nursing their wounds, she used her pain to discover her voice and speak up for her rights and the rights of blacks and women. Strengthened by her faith, and with the help of some white friends, Sojourner took the man who sold her child into slavery to court and won. The case securing her son's emancipation was one of the first in which a black woman successfully challenged a white man in a United States court.

While there are many more women I could write about, I cannot bring this chapter to a close without talking about Elisabeth Elliot. Elisabeth had been married for only twenty-seven months when she experienced tragedy. In 1956, her husband, Jim, was one of five missionaries speared to death while attempting to bring the gospel to the Auca/Waodani tribe in Ecuador. Two years later, still in the midst of incredible heartache and pain, Elisabeth returned with her toddler to live among and minister to the people who had killed her husband. Such an act of forgiveness and love is almost too much for us to comprehend. When asked about how to deal with hurt, Elisabeth responded that first you need to "receive God's grace." It's God's grace that works in our hearts to receive God's forgiveness and give us the ability to forgive others. It helps to meditate on Colossians 3:12–14, where Paul instructs us "as God's chosen people, holy and dearly loved,

---

* Olive Gilbert and Sojourner Truth, *Narrative of Sojourner Truth, a Bondswoman of Olden Time* (Battle Creek, Mich., 1878), pp. 302–3.

clothe yourselves with compassion, kindness, humility, gentleness and patience. Bear with each other and forgive one another if any of you has a grievance against someone. Forgive as the Lord forgave you. And over all these virtues put on love, which binds them all together in perfect unity" (NIV). Just as we have been forgiven by Christ, we are called to forgive others. As followers of Jesus, we are to be clothed in attire that represents Him. Instead of putting on garments of impatience, pride, selfishness, and hostility, we are called to walk in love and grace. It might help to think of it this way: After doing an intense cardio workout, you go shower and get dressed in clean clothes. None of us put on the sweaty, stinky clothes we worked out in. God has forgiven us and made us clean. As recipients of His grace, we do not want to put on the foul-smelling clothes of unforgiveness. By His grace, He has forgiven us and given us the ability to forgive others.

After receiving God's grace to forgive, Elisabeth would say next it's important to "acknowledge the wrong." Forgiving doesn't mean you are excusing what someone said or did. Forgiveness is a process that allows you to no longer be bound by what happened. Thus, it's important to acknowledge the wrong. I encourage you to be straightforward with God. That's exactly what Paul did in his letter to Timothy. He wrote about how "Alexander the metalworker did me a great deal of harm. The Lord will repay him for what he has done" (2 Timothy 4:14 NIV). Notice that Paul was not looking to be the one to "repay" Alexander. Paul received God's grace and acknowledged the wrong done to him. He left it up to the Lord to "repay [Alexander] for what he has done." Which leads to the third thing Elisabeth said to do when asked how to forgive.

After receiving God's grace and acknowledging the wrong, third, we need to "lay down all rights." Forgiveness, she explained, is the "unconditional laying down of the self. This includes the desire for vindication, pleasure at the other person's humiliation, keeping accounts of evil, the right to an apology, and bringing every thought under obedience to Christ." Romans 12:19 tells us, "Do not take revenge, dear friends, but leave room for God's wrath. For it is written, 'Vengeance belongs to me. I will pay them back, declares the Lord'" (ISV).

And lastly in response to the one who has wronged you, Elisabeth says, "If they ask forgiveness, then we forgive." Colossians 3:13 instructs us to "Forgive as the Lord forgave you" (NIV). When Jesus began to teach his disciples and the crowds gathered to listen to him, he taught them how to pray. He instructed them to say a prayer of forgiveness. We learn we are to pray, "Forgive us our debts, as we also have forgiven our debtors." Jesus assured them, "If you forgive other people when they sin against you, your heavenly Father will also forgive you. But if you do not forgive others their sins, your Father will not forgive your sins" (Matthew 6:14 NIV).

After receiving God's grace, acknowledging the wrong, and laying down our rights, if the person who wronged us does not ask for forgiveness, then Elisabeth Elliot says we are to "forgive in a private conversation with God and pray for them." Forgiveness is just as much for us as for them. We are able to let go of emotions that have become heavy burdens. We can give the hurt to the Lord and receive His healing and peace. In order to put it all behind us and move forward, Elisabeth says to "ask God for the grace to treat them as if nothing had ever come between you." She found it helpful to reflect on Psalm 119:78: "May the arrogant be put to shame for wronging me without cause; but I will meditate on your precepts" (NIV). Focusing on the commandments and instructions in the Word of God is what helps us continue to walk in forgiveness.

These women have weathered the storms of life and have overcome to be able to say that God is faithful. You can feel the weight of their faith, their strength, their authority, and their love. They have not only spoken and taught about forgiveness, they have lived it. Each woman coming from paths of immense pain and sorrow, brought together at the foot of the cross. There they found a Savior who loved them so much that He gave His life for them. His willingness to forgive all and take on the sins of the world so that we might have a relationship with the Father was their foundation for forgiveness. I believe if you or I had the opportunity to meet any of these women, they would gently invite us to join them at the foot of the cross where Jesus died for you and for me. Long before we came into being, long before the abuse, the broken dreams, the betrayal, the cruel things said and done to us, long before all of that, He was there. And He wants us to bring our hurt, anger, pain, frustration, and sorrow to Him. I believe He would say:

I know you are hurting and feel so alone, like no one sees you, understands, or even cares. I love you. I see you. I care for you deeply. And I know you more than you know yourself. I am here for you. I would love for you to come and talk with Me. Let it all out—the screams, the tears, and the heartache. We will cry together. My heart breaks for what you went through. It was not My desire for that adult to come in the room and touch you; it was not My desire for the kids to torment you on the playground; it was not My will when your spouse left. It was not My will for Sojourner to go through that abuse, or for Corrie and her family to be put in the concentration camps, for Jarena to experience such discrimination, or Elisabeth's husband to be murdered. My heart broke as they went through those horrible things that sin brought into the world. That was not what I wanted for them, nor is what you went through what I desired for you. I want you to experience true love, joy, and peace. I want you to live in the freedom I gave My life for you to receive. Will you do as these women did and bring me all your hurt, bitterness, anger, heartache, and sorrow?

I want to take that from you and give you My love, My joy, and My peace, so that you can experience true healing and life. Let Me take care of the person who hurt you. Would you release them and what they did and give it to Me? I want you to begin to experience true freedom and live the life I designed for you to live. I want you to walk in your purpose and flourish. Those who have gone before you discovered that it was through forgiveness that they were able to embrace their destiny.

Because Jarena forgave and let go, in 1819 she became the first African-American woman authorized to preach in the African Methodist Episcopal Church. She was also the first African-American woman to have an autobiography published in the United States. When challenged by skeptics about being a female minister, she responded, "Did not Mary first preach the risen Savior?"* Jarena overcame the racial and gender barriers of her time and became a trailblazer for women in ministry.

Because Corrie ten Boom forgave, she and her sister led many other prisoners to Christ. It is estimated that around eight hundred Jews were saved by the Ten Boom family's efforts. It's fascinating to note that the Dutch prefix "ten" means "at the" and "Boom" means "tree." The Ten Boom family "tree" became a place of refuge for so many whose lives were in danger. Does that imagery sound familiar? Doesn't it make you think of the verse we discussed earlier in this chapter? Jeremiah 17:7–8 assures us, "Blessed is the one who trusts in the Lord, whose confidence is in him. They will be like a tree planted by the water that sends out its roots by the stream. It does not fear when heat comes; its leaves are always green. It has no worries in a year

---

* Paul Harvey, *Through the Storm, Through the Night: A History of African American Christianity* (Lanham, Md.: Rowman and Littlefield Publishers, 2011), p. 43.

of drought and never fails to bear fruit" (NIV). The roots of the Ten Boom "tree" were planted by the water in good soil and as a result they produced fruit that long outlived them.

Corrie's experiences led her to thirty-three years of ministry in more than sixty countries, where she spoke about forgiveness and Christ's love. She wrote numerous books, including *The Hiding Place*, in which she told the story of her family members and their World War II work. Her book has been read by millions worldwide, was adapted into a movie, and became one of the most successful Christian films ever produced. Because Corrie was so transparent about what it was like to meet and forgive one of the prison guards who had held her captive, so many others have been encouraged to also forgive.

Because Sojourner Truth forgave, she did not stay trapped by the wrongs that had been done to her and her son. She walked in her purpose and blazed a trail for countless numbers who have come after her. She traveled the country preaching the gospel and giving speeches on racial and gender inequalities. In 1864 Sojourner was invited to meet President Abraham Lincoln. After the Civil War, she worked to improve conditions for former slaves. She dedicated her life to the needs of African-Americans and women, including abolition, voting rights, and property rights. Although she never learned to read or write, her life's work and legacy continue to be written about, read, and honored by generations. Sojourner Truth was posthumously inducted into the National Women's Hall of Fame and included in the Smithsonian Institution's list of the "100 Most Significant Americans." In 1986, the US Postal Service issued a commemorative stamp in her honor. In 1997, NASA dedicated its Mars Pathfinder Rover after her. In 2014, an asteroid was named in her honor. And in 2009, a bust of Sojourner Truth was installed in the US Capitol, making her the first black woman to be honored with a statue in the Capitol building.

Because Elisabeth Elliot forgave, so many others have been inspired to forgive, love, and serve those we never thought possible. Because Elisabeth not only forgave the Waodani, but went and lived with them, many among their tribe and eventually around the world accepted Christ as a result of her ministry. Elisabeth's story shines brightly in a culture where we cancel, ghost, and ice people for far less significant offenses. Elisabeth wrote about her life experiences in her numerous classics, including *Through Gates of Splendor*, *Shadow of the Almighty*, *Joyful Surrender*, *Passion and Purity*, *Let Me Be a Woman*, and *Suffering Is Never for Nothing*. Along with being a missionary to Ecuador, Elisabeth went on to become a critically acclaimed speaker, professor, contributor to the NIV Bible translation, author of over thirty books, and the host of a daily radio program for twelve years.

I hope the stories of these remarkable women inspired you. My desire is that by sharing stories of others who have also gone through incredibly painful experiences, you would know you are not alone. That you would see that while it is so difficult to forgive, there is so much good that can come out of it. I know it might not seem possible to forgive the person or people who hurt you. They have caused years of heartache, deep wounds, and scars. *They* should be the ones asking you for forgiveness. I know it seems so unfair that after all they did to you, you have to be the one to forgive them. But it's the only way to freely move forward with your life. I'm not saying you need to go have a conversation with them to forgive. That might not be safe or wise in certain situations. What I'm talking about is forgiving them in your heart. Because refusing to forgive them is imprisoning you in your past. It's giving them even more power and control over you. It's continuing their legacy of destruction in your life. It's also preventing you from truly healing, as you continue to pick at the open wound. As the saying goes, refusing to forgive is like drinking poison and expecting the other person to die. In other words, when you hold on to bitterness and anger, the only person you end up hurting is yourself. And instead of flourishing, you will begin to decay.

There is so much more that can be said on the subject of forgiveness, but I hope you have been inspired to begin the process. There will need to be more work done to bring healing, and as it is not the sole topic of this book, I encourage you to supplement this chapter with additional resources, books, support groups, or professional counseling. In later chapters, we will discuss the value of bringing others into the journey of healing. This includes healthy friends, small groups that focus on healing, pastors, and professional counselors. For now, I will leave you with this question: What could be possible as you make the decision to forgive? What might not happen if you decide it's too hard to forgive and let go of the past? While we can't fully know the extent of each answer, it does give us something to seriously consider. It's important to acknowledge that while each of the four women we discussed were doing notable things, it was after they forgave the person(s) who hurt them, that they each stepped into a deeper level of purpose. It unlocked things and set others into motion. I believe there is so much more waiting for you on the other side of your decision to forgive. Letting go of offenses allows you to experience freedom, peace, clarity, and focus. No longer will you be consumed by the past, but instead you will be open to what the future holds. I believe in you and I'm cheering you on as you take steps toward freedom, walking in your purpose, and flourishing.

CHAPTER 2

Gluing Leaves
on Trees

I remember the day my elementary school teacher handed out a piece of paper with an outline of a large tree to each student in our class. There were no leaves on the branches, so I thought we were going to color them in. But instead of telling us to take out our crayons, she gave each of us a small bag of red, orange, and yellow tissue papers, cut into one-inch squares. She instructed us to take a piece of tissue paper and fold it over the top of our pencils. Then we were to add a small drop of glue to the tissue paper and stick it on the tree to create 3D leaves. We were to continue doing that until the tree was full of red, orange, and yellow leaves. I got to work on this new and unusual assignment of gluing leaves on my tree, making sure the different colors were evenly dispersed. What started as a blank white sheet of paper with only the outline of a tree eventually turned into a colorful masterpiece. This was a beautiful project to do as a child in elementary school. However, it's not pretty when we try to do the same thing in real life as adults.

In the previous chapter, we discussed things in our heart that we need to let go. This chapter focuses on the things in our mind that we need to release. Certain thoughts, patterns, beliefs, and "pictures" in our heads that have become part of our fiber and are preventing us from growing. It's the stories we've told ourselves and the lies we've believed. The ones spoken over us by so-called friends, family, complete strangers, or even ourselves. Over the years, they were absorbed through our root systems and have become so ingrained, it's hard to separate the lies from the truth. Letting go of things in our mind also includes releasing dreams of how we envisioned our lives would look like. The idyllic "picture" in our head of how we had expected life to be. We try, often to our detriment, to make something happen when living in the tension between the current reality and unfulfilled dreams. Like the childhood art project, we desperately try to glue things back on and retain some form of the picture we created in our minds. We hold on to the person we're dating, even when we know they're not good for us, because we believe it's better than being alone. We hold on to our money, even though we've been taught that the tithe belongs to the Lord, because we can't see how that principle applies to anyone in our current financial situation. We did the math and it just doesn't add up or make sense. We hold on to the untruths about who we are and what we are able to accomplish that were spoken over us as a child, giving them the power to still cripple us today in the midst of a successful career. We hold on to the dream to have a family that seems to be slipping away with each passing year. I'm not saying that we shouldn't dream. We all need to do that. However, we cannot put our lives on hold while we are believing for our miracle. Sometimes we need to adjust the dream or let go of it in order to live and embrace a new vision or purpose for our lives. We may need to adjust who we are surrounding ourselves with, who we are "following," or who we are letting speak into our lives.

There are relationships, beliefs, and expectations we are holding on to that are preventing us from flourishing. Not everyone is supposed to go into the next season of your life with you. That next level that you are going to requires a new way of thinking and operating. Your old habits and thought patterns are not going to work. What you previously relied on is no longer going to be able to sustain you. You need to be okay with letting go of the familiar and comfortable in order to embrace the new. We need to let go and not attempt to "glue" the leaves back onto the tree.

Trees don't try to pick up their leaves once they've fallen. Instead, the fallen leaves decompose and become rich soil, providing nutrients for the tree to keep growing. In the same way, as we let go of unhealthy things in our lives, they fall to the ground and decompose to provide nutrients that make us stronger. My friend, God does not waste anything. As you let go, He is using those leaves to create the topsoil and fertilizer that will provide nutrients to help you remain planted and flourish during the winter season. I can say that with confidence because I've experienced it throughout my life.

One of the first times I remember going to the mall was in elementary school. My mom had taken me with her when she went shopping with one of her friends. As they made their way through the aisles of clothes, I busied myself by watching people shop, making sure to stay within earshot of my mom's voice. At some point, I got the feeling someone was watching me. I turned around and spotted a little boy who looked a couple years younger than I was. He seemed puzzled as he stared at me. His tousled light brown hair partially covered his green eyes. His red T-shirt and blue jean shorts were a sharp contrast against his pale skin. As he continued to intently gawk at me, I gazed back, determined not to lose this impromptu staring contest. We locked eyes for what seemed like a long time. I thought I had won the challenge when he finally began to squirm. But before I could turn away, he pointed toward me while tugging on his mom's pants and said, "Mommy, why is her skin so dirty? Didn't she take a bath?"

I turned to see who he was pointing at, but there was no one behind me. I looked back at him and his voice got louder as he asked his mom the same question again. I glanced down at my legs to see if I had dropped some food on them. My white cotton shorts with pastel stripes hung just above my knees, revealing my dark legs. There was nothing on them. I held out my arms and looked them over carefully. Except for my ashy elbows, my skin looked clean. My eyes widened as I realized the boy was asking why my skin was dark brown, the color of dirt, and not white and "clean" like his. I looked back over at the boy and then up at his mother. There was an awkward silence as she tried to divert his attention. I listened to see how she was going to respond to his question. She did not say anything to me, nor did she answer her son. Instead, she firmly grabbed his arm and said, "Let's go."

"But, Mom, why doesn't she have to take a bath? Why do you always make me take one?" the boy whined while looking back at me as she rushed him out of the store.

"Shhhh!" I could hear her whisper as she hurried him along.

I stood all alone in the aisle wondering what just happened. Why would he think that my skin was dirty? I took a bath today.

"Grraaaace," Mom called suddenly, snapping me out of my train of thought, "where are you?"

I quickly went to where she was and stood quietly beside her, not sure if I should tell her what had just happened.

"Where have you been? It's not safe for you to wander off like that. I need you to stay here with me where I can see you. We'll be done soon."

I followed her around the store, all the while looking at my skin. Mom finally finished her shopping and we left the mall.

When we got home, I went straight to the bathroom, determined to wash off any "dirt" from my skin. I wanted to make sure what the little boy had said was not true. I turned on the faucet, stuck my arms in the sink, and began to wash them using a bar soap and a washcloth. I scrubbed harder, looking for dirt or any sign of "cleaner" skin underneath; but nothing happened. After some time, my skin was still dark brown and my arm was raw from all the rubbing.

"Grace, are you okay in there?" Mom asked, knocking on the door.

"Yes," I meekly replied, reaching for a towel.

"You've been in there quite a while," she stated. "What are you doing?"

"Nothing," I said. "I'm fine."

I quickly dried my arms and hung the towel on the bar, knowing at any moment, Mom was going to open the door to see what I was doing. I straightened up the bathroom and went to my room.

I wish I could go back in time and speak to the young girl in the bathroom. I'd gently have her put down the bar of soap, take both of her hands in mine, and have her turn and look at me. I would say: "Beautiful girl, you are not dirty. You are a masterpiece of incredible value and worth. You are made in the image of God. There will be people who will try to make you feel dirty, dumb, ugly, and unwanted. But you must not listen to those small, insecure voices. They might tease you for your dark skin and thick lips, but years from now, they will be putting on self-tanner to get some color and injecting collagen in their lips to make them as stunning as yours. Know who you are and hold your head up high. You are a daughter of the King. Embrace your natural hair as a royal crown. Take your place. You have authority, you have the mind of Christ, you were made in His image, and He has amazing plans for your life. You are chosen and called by the Creator of the universe to do great things. There is nothing anyone can do to stop the good work God has started in you. He is going to complete it. He is with you and will fight your battles. He has commanded his angels to watch over you wherever you go. This is all true for you too, my friend. It is our identity and promise as children of God. The enemy knows the freedom and power that comes with embracing our identity in Christ. That's why he does everything he can to prevent us from discovering who we truly are, our incredible worth and God-given authority. He knows it unlocks the door to us walking in our purpose and truly flourishing. And so, he does everything he can to keep us deceived."

Sadly, it would be years before that young girl realized her true identity, beauty, and value. Instead, the little boy's question was the first of many times she was called names: Buckwheat, oreo, white-washed, cotton hair, and nigger.

As the list of labels grew throughout junior high and into high school, I struggled to find my identity. I knew what they were saying was not who I was. At the same time, I didn't have an answer of my own. I wrestled with the question: Who am I? It was unsettling to realize I did not know. I remember gazing at my reflection in my bedroom mirror, wondering why I was here. It was as if a stranger with brown almond-shaped eyes was staring back at me. "Lord," I whispered, "some people say I am this, and others say I am that; but I want to know what You say about me. Who do You say I am?" I stood there for a long time, hoping to get some type of response that would help me understand and make sense of it all. In the silence, I closed my eyes, searching for what to do next as I wiped the tears off my cheeks.

I thought I might find something in the Bible. I didn't know what I was looking for as I picked up my black leather-bound New International Version and sat on my bed. Wiping the tears from my eyes, I prayed for God to reveal an answer to my question. The book of Isaiah had a well-known encouraging verse at the end of the fortieth chapter, so I decided to start reading there. When I got to Isaiah 41:9 and read, "I took you from the ends of the earth, from its farthest corners I called you. I said 'You are my servant'; I have chosen you and have not rejected you," it was as if God was speaking directly to me. According to the verse, He had chosen me! Unlike what I had experienced from others at school, He had picked me! I read the verse over and over, thinking about what it meant to be chosen by God. It wasn't like junior high PE when two different captains took turns choosing people for their team, often resulting in lower self-esteem for those of us who were selected toward the end. God's selection process is not like that. You and I are God's first pick. Jesus forgave our sins and gave His life so that we can have a relationship with God who has chosen us.

In the following days, I continued to search my Bible, looking for new truths about my identity. I flipped through the New Testament and noticed several verses I had previously highlighted. "The Spirit himself testifies with our spirit that we are God's children. Now if we are children, then we are heirs—heirs of God and co-heirs with Christ" (Romans 8:16–17). I paused and thought about the words I had just read and what they meant. They revealed I was a child of God, and not only that, but I was also His heir! I had never heard anyone tell me I was an heir.

"I am a child of God," I said out loud, staring at the words on the page. "I am an heir of God."

I said the words slowly, letting them roll off my tongue while treasuring the meaning of what I was saying. I felt like something in my world had shifted. If God was my Father, that meant He was looking out for me as a loving parent looks out for their kid. While I realized it didn't mean God was going to zap the playground bullies with a lightning bolt, I felt comforted and safe knowing He had my back. According to the verse, not only was I a child of God, I was also an heir of God. I had never met an heiress, but from the little I understood, they inherit everything their parents own. I wondered, as I continued flipping through the pages of my Bible, if that could be true for me. I turned to the book of Psalms, and started reading at Psalm 91. I knew it was a chapter in which my parents had found encouragement and hope. I continued reading until I got to Psalm 95:3: "For the LORD is the great God, the great King above all gods." The words seemed to jump off the page as I began to connect the dots from the passages I had been reading. *If God is King, and I am a child of God, then that must make me a…*I paused as I realized the revelation…*a princess!*

I sat transfixed, unsure what to do with what I'd just discovered. I tried saying the words out loud to see how they would sound. "I…am…a princess," I said slowly, letting each word sink in. They seemed so surreal.

I waited in silence as if expecting a confirmation from heaven. I knew it had to be true since God would not tell a lie. "Wow! I'm royalty," I said as I sat up straight.

It was as if my unknown identity had suddenly been revealed. Slipping off my bed, I walked to the mirror, squared my shoulders, lifted my chin, and said out loud, "I am a child of the King." The girl looking back at me did not look like any of the princesses I had seen on TV or in the movies. But that did not matter. I knew I was on to something. My parents and Sunday School teachers had told me that God loved me. But in this moment, I was discovering how God *saw* me. And it was radically different from what the kids on the elementary school playground and in my middle school classes had said.

I was not a disheveled character named Buckwheat. "I am a child of God," I repeated out loud. "I am chosen by God." I continued to repeat those words while staring into the mirror, each time grasping more of their reality.

"Dinner's ready!" A voice from the kitchen drew me out of my royal ballroom. I walked down the hall, knowing that while I did not have all the answers, something significant had just taken place.

Learning what God had to say about my identity planted seeds of healing and stirred a sense of empowerment. In the following weeks and months, I combed through the pages of the Bible, soaking up the truths it contained about who I was. As I learned how the God of the Universe saw me, it transformed how I saw myself. My confidence grew and I slowly began to accept my uniqueness rather than trying so hard to fit in. God chose me for who I was. Not for what I could do or what I looked like. Just for who I was.

The ramifications of that childhood trip to the mall and the names I was called in the school years long after required a lot of releasing and letting go. Not only did I have to release the anger and hurt toward the boy for what he said, but also toward his mom for not saying anything in response. There were so many life-giving ways she could have responded, so many ways she could have set me on a whole different path. If only she had responded to her son within my hearing: "She is not dirty." Imagine the difference that would have made! As painful as that encounter was, I realize it was a catalyst that led me to do a deep dive into discovering my identity at an early age. That enabled me to establish a solid foundation as my roots grew deep into the Word of God.

Through the process, I realized that I not only had to release the anger and hurt I had but I also had to release their lies that had infiltrated my head. Their poisonous words had seeped into my heart and mind, causing me to wither. Many of us need to let go of negative beliefs we've absorbed—whether from others or ourselves. Some of us may need to let go of a dream that is well past its prime or may not have been for us in the first place. Others of us need to let go of the unhealthy thoughts, patterns, and narratives we have embraced as truth. I know it's not easy to do that, but if you stick with me for the next few pages, you will see how this is all vital in preparation for the upcoming seasons.

We need to release the lies that have been spoken over us. Maybe you were told you were an accident, a mistake, or a failure. Maybe you were constantly compared to the model sibling and reminded of how you did not measure up or were not going to amount to anything. Maybe you were told that "it" was your fault—whether it was the abuse, the divorce, the accident. I am so sorry for the lies that were spoken over you. I'm sorry for the amount of hurt, pain, and deep wounds they caused. Just like I wish I could take the hands of the little girl trying to wash off her "dirty" skin and instead speak words of love and life into her, I wish I could do the same for you at the age when you first heard those ugly words. I wish I could wipe away the tears and cancel whatever lie was said and replace it with life-giving truth. But I have found that there is someone who, even more than me, understands your pain and wants to bring healing. In this fall season of letting go, God wants to help you release the lies that have been spoken over you and replace them with His truth.

I want you to know the truth that you are God's masterpiece. You are one of a kind. You are an original design of incredible value and worth. You are uniquely gifted and talented. No one has the same fingerprints as you. No one else will be able to leave the unique imprint on this earth that you will. No one else will be able to do what you were created to do. Your superpower is the authority you have as a follower of Christ. Jesus said, "I have given you authority to trample on snakes and scorpions and to overcome all the power of the enemy" (Luke 10:19 NIV). You have the ability to override the lies and negative thought patterns. God wants to reveal to you the truth about your identity, your purpose, and who you are uniquely designed to be. The main place you will find that is in the words He wrote, in the Bible. I know it can be somewhat intimidating and confusing to figure out how to read the Word of God and understand how it applies to your life. But don't worry, I got you covered.

I did something on my journey of discovery that was so simple and easy to do, but incredibly impactful and empowering. I think you might find it helpful, too.

All you need to do is get a blank piece of paper and draw a line down the middle. On the left side, write down the lies that have been spoken over you by others or yourself. Lies like, "I'm not going to make it…I don't have anything to offer…I'm not beautiful…No one sees me…I don't have what it takes…" Write down as many as you can think of on one side of the page, leaving space between each statement.

Next, we need to begin to replace the lies we wrote down with life-giving truth. We need to discover what God says. So take the list you created and ask God, "This is what people have said about me and what I've come to believe about myself. I want to know what You say about me." Then find a Bible (I recommend using something easy to read like the NIV, ESV, or NLT versions) and ask the Lord to show you the truth of who you are through His Word. For example, according to His Word, you are more than a conqueror (see Romans 8:37), and you can do all things through Christ who strengthens you (see Philippians 4:13). For those of you who are not as familiar with the Bible, I created a resource with some of the most common lies we believe and the truths that you can replace them with. You can find that resource on my website: www.gratitudewithgrace.com. You can also go on biblegateway.com and type in a specific word and it will pull up all the verses that include that word. For example, if you type in "fear," one of the 336 verses that come up is 2 Timothy 1:7: "For God has not given us a spirit of fear, but of power and of love and of a sound mind" (NKJV). If sorting through hundreds of verses seems a little overwhelming, just start with the resource I mentioned and build from there. As you find the truth statement that applies to each lie, write it on the right side of the paper. You may not finish this project in one sitting, but I encourage you to set aside some time to complete it.

When you're done, take the list and stand in front of a mirror. Look yourself in the eye and read the first truth statement out loud. I know it may seem awkward at first. But think about all the times you've stood in front of the same mirror and said all types of negative things about yourself. We are going to begin to release that toxicity. Continue reading the rest of the truth statements out loud to your reflection in the mirror. It may feel like the words you are saying do not describe who you see, but I encourage you to stick with it. Rewiring our thoughts and words takes some time. But as you keep at it, it will begin to feel more natural. You might even want to add some more truth statements that come to mind! Repeat all of them until you have memorized as many as you can. Absorb them into your soul like roots soaking in nutrients for a tree. Continue to repeat them until you begin to believe what you are saying. As you consistently declare the truths over yourself, you will begin to see who you are created to be. Chosen, loved, a masterpiece.

This process takes time and can be challenging because the untrue statements have been with us for so long and are often ingrained in the fiber of our being. It may be helpful to remind yourself that just as the process of leaves falling and beginning to decay takes time, so does releasing things we have believed for many years. But the reward of sticking with the process is incredibly worth it. As leaves decompose, they become rich soil, providing nutrients for the tree to keep growing. In the same way, as you release the lies, thoughts, and negative beliefs, they, too, will decompose and become rich soil to make you stronger. So I want to encourage you to press through the awkwardness of hearing yourself speak life-giving words out loud to yourself. As you do, you will be speaking in alignment with what God says about you. When He sees you, He sees someone beautiful, chosen, and valued. Not only does He see you as someone of incredible worth, He sees you as worth dying for. He does not agree with the lies spoken over you; He is not mad at you, judging you, or disappointed in you. Long before any person said anything to you or about you, God said you were His. He wants to help you peel back and release all those layers and discover who you really are. Who He created you to be.

I pray that as you take the time to do this exercise, you will begin to see transformation in your life. Replacing what was spoken over you with the truth from God's Word will enable you to walk in your purpose and truly flourish. I realize we went deep pretty fast. But it's only so we can get to the reason you picked up this book in the first place. You see, all of this ties together. Releasing things and letting go is connected to finding purpose and flourishing in your current season. It's like plants and shrubs—we all know that although it seems counterproductive, plants grow better after they have been pruned. The process may not be fun and it definitely does not look pretty, but in the end, that's when they truly flourish.

One of my hardest moments of letting go came unexpectedly a few years ago. It involved my health. I had been experiencing painful cramps, heavy bleeding, pressure, bloating, and constantly needing to urinate. Sorry if that's TMI, but it's what made me decide to go see my doctor. I found out my symptoms were due to a large number of benign tumors, called fibroids, in my uterus. After going through an abdominal myomectomy ten years ago to have them removed, they had now been replaced by new ones that were impacting every aspect of my life. I could deal with the weight gain and even make it through the extremely painful cramps. And while rather stressful, I had figured out safeguards to avoid accidents from the heavy bleeding each month. But it was the constant pressure, discomfort, and never-ending need to use the bathroom that wrecked me. What started as waking up once in the middle of the night to go to the bathroom turned into an endless season of sitting on my toilet instead of sleeping in our bed. It got to the point that I was having to rush to go relieve my bladder just before walking on stage to speak. The urge to go urinate would begin to build again halfway through my message and I would have to shorten my talk in order to avoid a public incident. I knew something had to be done.

I went to see my OB-GYN to discuss my options. She explained that I was at the equivalent of being five months pregnant, and the largest fibroid was pressing on my bladder, resulting in constantly having to urinate.

"Even if I go in and remove all the fibroids, because you are still young, they will likely grow back again. The only way to get rid of them completely is to do a hysterectomy."

"A *what?*" I responded in disbelief. "There has to be some other option! That can't be the solution!"

"I can remove the fibroids as a temporary solution. But if you want to no longer have them come back again, the only permanent solution is a hysterectomy." Her words sucked what little air there was out of the small exam room.

I stared at her, anxiously listening for another alternative. In the awkward silence, I slowly realized she was serious that removing my uterus was the only solution for complete relief. My chest began to heave and I struggled to breathe. Tears welled up in my eyes as I began to realize what this would mean. *This can't be happening.* I shook my head in denial. *There has got to be another option.* The room seemed to be spinning with pictures of babies she had delivered over several decades of her practice. The walls felt like they were closing in and about to crush me. I needed to get out and escape this new reality.

No windshield wipers could wipe the tears that gushed from within me as I drove home. My cries turned to wails as I gripped the steering wheel, attempting to hold on to something as my world crashed around me. Instead of wailing from the pain of childbirth, I was wailing because my childhood dream of birthing children had just been shattered. I would not hold a baby in my arms while my husband carried our toddler. There would be no way to glue the tissue paper leaves back on to the picture I created.

By the time I got home, my tears had turned to anger. So many questions raged in my mind, the loudest of which were "Why is this happening to *me?*...God, why aren't You *doing* something?" Another was, "Will I still be a woman?" I was terrified at the thought of removing something from my body that to me was the very essence of womanhood. For me, this was not like taking out a kidney, this was removing the very core of my femininity. Was I making a permanent decision I might someday regret? Removing the ability to create a human being, to raise a child and leave a legacy. While my OB-GYN said she was going to keep my ovaries intact for hormone balance, I really didn't want to hear it. I was mad that God had not healed me and that it had come to this. The first instruction He gave Adam and Eve was to "be fruitful and multiply" (Genesis 1:28 NLT). Clearly that was something He saw as important and special. And yet for some unknown reason, I was being excluded from that. Instead of carrying a child, I was carrying fibroids. And at the same time, I felt called to ministry. How could He expect me to speak when I was having to run to the bathroom every few *minutes?* If He wanted His message of the gospel to be shared with more people, why was He not doing something about this issue?

There were many sleepless nights leading up to the procedure. I wrestled with the fact that my reality was not matching the "tissue paper" picture I had created so long ago. From the days of playing "house" with Ken and Barbie and a slew of other dolls, this was not what I had imagined. As much as I tried to find other solutions, there were just no other viable options.

The "H" day eventually came, and long before the sun came up, Phil and I headed to the hospital. As I sat in the car agonizing over how my life was going to change, I asked the Lord for a word. By this point my anger had subsided and I had made peace with the fact that my healing from the fibroids would come through modern medicine rather than a divine miracle. It was not the way I would have chosen, but I recognized that He is still God and His ways are higher than my own. In the stillness of the car, I felt like the Lord asked me a question in response to my plea.

"Grace, when did you give Me your life?"

I immediately responded: "When I was a little girl."

To which He replied with another question: "Did that include your uterus?"

I looked down at my protruding belly. This was not part of the plan when I surrendered my life to Jesus. I figured that would involve loving Him, worshiping Him, and loving others. Relinquishing my uterus was nowhere in the picture I had envisioned. As followers of Christ, we say that we surrender our lives to the Lord, but I'd never heard anyone specifically mention her uterus. After all, when we talk about surrendering to the Lord, we often refer to our careers, our future, our plans, or our finances. But in that moment, I realized that when I surrendered my life to the Lord, it meant *all* of me, including my uterus.

So after a lengthy pause, I slowly let the air out of my lungs and answered, "Yes."

Phil and I sat in silence as we drove down the empty road on this unexpected and unknown journey. I definitely did not expect to have my uterus removed, and I did not know how it was going to affect me mentally, emotionally, physically. And yet in the midst of all that, I felt like the Lord was with me. While His way was not what I'd expected and definitely did not make sense to me, I knew that I could trust Him. He had been with me time and time again. Through the good times and the hard times. He never let go. And I knew He wasn't about to start now.

I cupped both of my hands over my belly and felt the hard lump of a large mass. As the oldest of five kids, I had felt my mom's stomach when she was pregnant with each of my younger siblings as they started to move and kick. I had looked forward to rubbing my own belly and experiencing a child growing inside me. However, instead of having the opportunity to feel a baby kick, I felt the hard lump of a large mass. Looking down at my protruding abdomen, I took a deep breath and uttered words I never thought I would ever say. "Lord, this is not what I pictured for my uterus." I sighed heavily. "But Lord, all I am, all of me, including each of my organs, belongs to You. I give You my uterus. And as I do, I'm believing that through it You are going to birth more in the spiritual than I would in the natural." We rode in silence the rest of the way to the hospital. Although everything in me did not want to let go of this special organ in my body, I felt an unexplainable peace in releasing it into the hands of the One who had created it.

That was one of the hardest prayers I have uttered in my faith journey. It was a new depth of surrender that my root system had not reached before. It is there I discovered soil comprised of rich nutrients. It was not manufactured potting soil from a bag created with human hands. Nor was it topsoil where nutrients for most trees are found. This was a deeper, more substantive soil. Although it was rare and unique, there were traces that seemed vaguely familiar. It reminded me of the time in college when I felt God calling me into full-time ministry and I surrendered my plan to become a doctor. As I continued to absorb the nutrients from the soil, I realized they were created by the things I had previously let go over time. Letting go of my dream to become a doctor was a difficult decision I'd wrestled with for about a year. Once

I finally released it and embraced my calling into ministry, I began to live out my purpose. I found that what I experienced after I released my dream and embraced His purpose was so much more fulfilling than I could have imagined. Absorbing those nutrients helped give me the strength to let go. And through the process, my spiritual roots grew deeper and stronger.

Sometimes we need to give ourselves space to grieve after letting go of something. The reality is my emotions were all over the place after the procedure. Not only was I on heavy pain meds, but I was also assigned a post-op room on the same floor as women who had had a C-section delivery. Early on, one of the nurses came in and asked about my baby. I wanted to snap at her for not thoroughly reading my chart before walking in and adding fuel to an already emotional situation. In a counseling session shortly afterward, my therapist explained that the feelings I was having were feelings of grief because I had just gone through a loss. Not only physically but also the loss of a dream. I needed to give myself grace to grieve that.

Some of you may need to do the same. Perhaps you thought you would be married by now, have children by now, have your own home, or have launched that business or ministry by now. Maybe you didn't expect to get pregnant, you didn't expect to fall sick, you didn't expect to have financial challenges, you didn't expect for your marriage and family to fall apart, you didn't expect to lose the business. Your reality does not look like the beautiful picture you had created in your mind. And gluing tissue paper leaves back onto the tree is not working. You might consider taking some time to ask God for wisdom regarding what you had envisioned. Is it something you are to hold on to or to release? I know it's a scary question because sometimes we don't want to know the answer. But if it is time to let it go, you can trust that He always has something better for you. It often may not look like what we anticipate, but it is what we need. Give yourself grace and allow yourself to grieve throughout the process. Take some time and have it out with the Lord if you need to. The Bible says to pour out your heart to Him. He is not shocked or upset by your anger or frustration. He will not love you any less. Let it all out. Tell Him how you really feel. He wants to be with you as you process your thoughts and emotions.

Then let's take that first step to let go of a particular dream or expectation. You may consider doing it in a way that is symbolic or meaningful to you. You might take some time to grieve, mourn, or cry with a friend. You might write it down and then rip the paper into shreds or burn it. You might go to counseling. Find what works for you and trust that as you let it go, God's got you. You are finding a new faith that will sustain and empower you through the seasons of life.

1 Corinthians 15:36 explains that "A seed must die before it can sprout from the ground" (CEV). The New Living Translation puts it this way: "When you put a seed into the ground, it does not grow into a plant unless it dies first." In other words, the seed, which contains the fullest potential of life, dies so that the plant can grow. New life is created from the death of the seed. In order for the plant to grow and eventually produce fruit, the seed must die. I wonder what things may need to be released in our lives so that we can grow. Seeds left in their packets in seed form will never realize their true purpose and flourish. When we bury all of ourselves—our hopes, dreams, and very being—in Him, we experience true surrender. As we die to ourselves, God creates new life and purpose in us.

We have a choice whether we are going to embrace that or continue to try and avoid it. God is not going to force you to surrender or let go of anything. It needs to be something that you chose to do. While letting go of things may not be something we look forward to, we can trust that there is more on the side than we can currently see. When a seed is buried, all it sees and experiences is darkness and isolation. After it dies, it begins to grow and eventually sprout. Suddenly it is exposed to light, animals, and other trees. After some time, it bears fruit. Because the original seed died, others are able to enjoy the fruit from the tree. What you are releasing and letting go is not just for you, but for your children and grandchildren, even if they are not born yet. There is more than you and I can imagine on the other side of our obedience and surrender to the Lord. Even though we can't see it yet, we can trust that "he who began a good work in you will carry it on to completion until the day of Christ Jesus" (Philippians 1:6 NIV). That is what I reflected on in the car as I buried my "seed" on the way to the hospital. While having a hysterectomy was not part of my plan, I assured myself that God had started a good work in my life and He was going to continue it. And while aspects of it did not make sense to me, I knew that He was in control. He had been providing for trees each season, year after year for centuries. In fact, He promised that "As long as the earth endures, seedtime and harvest, cold and heat, summer and winter, day and night will never cease" (Genesis 8:22 NIV). I believe the Lord has and will continue to honor the prayer of surrender I said that morning. That story is still being written with each new day. And you are part of it! The fact that you are reading this book and allowing me to share some of my journey with you is an answer to that prayer. My hope is that between the stories and the practical steps I've shared, you have found the courage to let go of the lies that have held you back and release the dreams that you've clung to into God's hands.

CHAPTER 3

The Altar in the Open House

Shortly after Phil and I got married, we began looking for a home. We enjoyed going to open houses and discussing what we liked or did not like about the property and the neighborhoods. One day, we went with our realtor to look at a particular house in a quiet established neighborhood. As we walked through the house, we could tell the owners had taken meticulous care of the home. The walls, windows, and floors were immaculately clean. There was not a single cobweb, dent, or scratch to be found. The cabinetry, appliances, fixtures, and hardware were all good quality. It was looking like we had found a great property...until we went outside. On the side of the carefully manicured lawn was an arbor lined with greenery covering a roughly five-foot-by-six-foot area. The ground was laid with stone tiles about a foot wide. Underneath the arbor was something neither of us had seen in all our years of looking at properties. There, under the shade of the foliage, was a large altar! Based on the outlined discoloration on top of the altar, there had been a sizable statue/god positioned on top of it. Neither the altar nor the entire enshrined area would be an easy thing to remove. There was a reason the previous owner had left it there! Given the time and cost it would take, we decided to move on to other properties.

Throughout history, altars have been used for religious offerings, sacrifices, and worship. In the Old Testament of the Bible, altars were places of personal encounters with God. The altar of incense was a place to worship and praise God. Some altars were built as a place of covenant or agreement. Others were places of intercession, forgiveness, and mighty acts of God. The most significant altar in the Bible was not a table or platform made of stone, marble, or gold. Rather, it was a cross made of wood. When Jesus died on the cross, He became the ultimate sacrifice. Because of His death and resurrection, we have forgiveness for our sins, the opportunity to be reconciled to God, and the promise of eternal life with Him. Because of what Jesus did, we no longer need to build physical altars and sacrifice animals. Instead, we are given new instructions in the New Testament. "So then, my friends, because of God's great mercy to us I appeal to you: Offer yourselves as a living sacrifice to God, dedicated to his service and pleasing to him. This is the true worship that you should offer" (Romans 12:1 GNT). I like how the Message paraphrase brings a unique perspective:

So here's what I want you to do, God helping you: Take your everyday, ordinary life—your sleeping, eating, going-to-work, and walking-around life—and place it before God as an offering. Embracing what God does for you is the best thing you can do for him. Don't become so well-adjusted to your culture that you fit into it without even thinking. Instead, fix your attention on God. You'll be changed from the inside out. Readily recognize what he wants from you, and quickly respond to it. Unlike the culture around you, always dragging you down to its level of immaturity, God brings the best out of you, develops well-formed maturity in you.

As followers of Christ, we build an "altar" in our hearts, and we are the sacrifice. This includes all of us, our bodies, our thoughts, emotions, plans, material things, relationships, future, etc. It is not easy to do, especially in our culture today when there is so much pressure to build a platform and expand your influence. However, so many of the teachings of Jesus are counter to the ways of the world. For example, "Whoever finds their life will lose it, and whoever loses their life for my sake will find it" (Matthew 10:39 NIV). "Love your enemies and pray for those who persecute you" (Matthew 5:44 NIV). And when it came to altars, Jesus' teaching continued to be counter to what was expected. To put it in today's culture, instead of building platforms, we need to build altars. Not physical altars, but rather altars in our hearts where we offer all we are as a living sacrifice. The altar is the place we encounter God in a deeper way.

I experienced that a few years before I was married when I decided to put all that I owned on the "altar." I had been meditating on Psalm 24:1: "The earth is the LORD's, and everything in it" (NLT). I reflected on the fact that everything I had came from God and ultimately was His. He had blessed me with a beautiful home and had entrusted me with the things I had. So, if I honestly believed this, I reasoned, then I should have no issue with letting go of something if He chose to entrust it to someone else. After mulling this over for some time, I decided to put it to a test. I wanted to know if there was anything in my life that I was holding on to more than Him. This came out of a place of laying everything on the altar, including my desire to be married.

About that time, three friends of mine were each looking to get a place of their own. I wanted to bless them by giving them items from my home I thought they would like and find useful in their apartments. As I rummaged through my kitchen, I thought, "This is going to be so great. Instead of having a garage sale, I'm going to give away the things I no longer need. I'll be getting rid of clutter, and they are getting things they can use in their new places." But as soon as I heard myself say that, I slowly set down the never-used serving dish I was holding and looked at the amassed items. I suddenly realized I was going about this all wrong. I was picking items that I wanted to get rid of or had no issue giving away. And if I picked the items, then I was selecting what I felt comfortable releasing. That was not truly letting go of *anything*. I knew I needed a new approach.

I decided to invite my friends to come to my house, each on a separate day. As I greeted the first friend at my front door, I shared why I had invited her over. "I've been meditating on Psalm 24:1 and 1 Corinthians 4:7, which say the earth is the Lord's and everything in it basically comes from Him and belongs to Him. I believe that includes everything He has given me. It all belongs to God. I'm grateful He entrusted me with the things for a season and I believe He now wants to entrust them to you. He wants you to have any of the items He has given me. So I would love for us to walk through each room in my house, and anything you see that you want, it's yours to take."

"What?" she asked, looking at me like I had lost my mind.

I repeated what I said.

"Wait, are you serious? I can take anything?"

"Yes, I'm serious. And yes, absolutely anything! Whatever you want is yours. The only thing is you need to take it with you when you leave. You can't come back later with a moving truck."

"Whoa," she said as it slowly began to sink in, and she glanced around my living room. I had no idea what to expect and neither did my friends.

They each cautiously picked their first item, testing to see if this was for real. They looked over at me and asked, "Is this okay?" They probably expected me to say, "Anything but that," and were surprised to hear, "Absolutely!" After a few more times of hearing "It's yours," and "Whatever you want," they got the hang of it. Suddenly, they were seeing the home they had visited on other occasions through a whole new lens. Instead of it being "Grace's home" and "Grace's things," it was the Lord's house and the Lord's things—things that He wanted them to have and enjoy.

Each friend focused on different items as they walked through the living room, the kitchen, my bedroom, the office, and the home gym. One was starting a new job and happened to be the same size as me, so she cleaned out my closet and took a large duffel bag full of clothes and accessories. Another focused on kitchen items and hesitantly took my KitchenAid mixer and an assortment of serving dishes, pots, and baking pans. The third friend focused on my home decor, including wall art, artificial plants, lamps, etc. I absolutely loved walking through the house and seeing their eyes light up as they saw something they wanted. I must admit, I had a slight moment of panic at one point when I realized my car keys were on the kitchen counter. If my car was taken, I wasn't sure how I was going to get to work; however, I figured God would work something out.

Over the course of a two-week period, the walls in my home became bare. The house became darker without lamps and candles. My cooking process had to be adjusted since I no longer had the use of certain tools, gadgets, cookware, and bakeware. It took me a little longer to find my spices without my spice rack. My closet was notably sparse, and it was a little challenging to mix and match outfits with the remaining clothes and jewelry. But none of that mattered because I was focused on something else. I wanted to live openhanded. To know there wasn't a "thing" I was holding on to more than God. I'm not saying it was easy. Especially since it was not the plan to go rush out and replace whatever they had taken. But through it all, I had found myself in a place where "things" were not more important to me than whatever God wanted, and I was elated! Essentially, everything in my house had been placed on the "altar," and I did not rush to take anything back. A huge part of the experience was learning to be content with what I had. I felt like I had moved a little closer to understanding what Paul wrote in Philippians 4:11 when he said, "I have learned to be content whatever the circumstances" (NIV).

I do not share this experience to boast or to suggest you invite people to walk through your home and take whatever they want. It's not something I have done again (although I did warn Phil that's the type of woman he was marrying). I share it to stir in our hearts a posture of surrender. To yield all that we are and all that we have to Him. To not hold on to anything the Lord may want us to let go of. To present ourselves to Him as empty vessels He can use for His purpose. To live a life where there is nothing that we want more than to be with the Lord and to please Him. Paul wrote in Philippians 2:21 that "everyone looks out for their own interests, not those of Jesus Christ" (NIV). I want to be someone who looks out for the interests of Jesus Christ. His interests always involve looking out for the interests of those He loves.

I know some of you are still wondering what happened after this experience. I continued to live with gratitude, content with what I had, and trusting Him to provide for my needs. I continued to live openhanded while stewarding the things that He had entrusted me with. Out of that experience, there's a little test I developed and have put into practice. Before I buy something, I ask myself, "If the Lord has me release this and give it to someone else, will I be okay with it?" If the answer is no, then I'm not ready to purchase it and be entrusted with it. I've found being able to let go and release whatever God says to creates space for Him to do great things. There is something so beautiful that happens when we let go of whatever we are holding on to so tightly. We begin to flourish. As you read this chapter, is there something that's coming to mind that you might need to release? Is there something He's nudging you to let go of during this fall season? In Exodus 20:3–4, God instructs us, "You shall have no other gods before me. You shall not make for yourself an image in the form of anything in heaven above or on the earth beneath or in the waters below" (NIV).

While most of us may not have an altar with a statue of a god in our backyard, the reality is, we may have something similar in our heart and mind. It could be money, cars, clothes, shoes, gadgets, etc. Or it can be things that monopolize our time. It's hard to have space for something new when we are consumed with what everyone else is doing. The Israelites chose to give their attention to a golden calf. That didn't turn out so well. God Himself admits, "I, the LORD your God, am a jealous God" (Exodus 20:5 NIV). He wants our complete, undivided devotion.

In Chapter 1, we talked about how leaves fall off deciduous trees so that the trees can survive the winter. We learned that the trees would die if their leaves were to remain on them. We've worked through letting go of offenses and hurts from the past. We've talked about letting go of unhealthy friendships and relationships that are not God's best for us, and about the lies that were spoken over us that told us false stories about who we truly are. But what about the *things* we hold on to so tightly?

How do we release material things and finances? I recognize that is not something that comes easily for everyone. Maybe because it was not role-modeled for us, or perhaps you may not have experienced the joy and fulfillment that comes from it. I thought I would share some things that might help you embrace the process.

See the beauty in letting go

Without this, letting go turns into something we do begrudgingly, or we agonize, question, and regret afterward. Phil and I recently moved to Birmingham, Alabama. Having grown up for most of my life in California, the land of palm trees, I'd forgotten how breathtaking the fall season is. The tapestry of red, orange, and yellow leaves displays God's splendor and the beauty of his creation. It's significant to recognize His stunning masterpiece only happens as trees begin the process of letting go.

We have drawn a lot of insight from trees throughout this fall section, especially their leaves. We know that, at a basic level, their job is to turn sunlight into food for the trees. They produce chlorophyll (the green color we see), which captures the energy in sunlight, and they then make sugar that the tree can use for its own energy. As the days get shorter in autumn, less sunlight hits the tree and the leaves make less chlorophyll. We then begin to see the vibrant hues. Fun fact: The orange and yellow colors are actually in the leaves during spring and summer, but they only become visible as the amount of green chlorophyll in the leaves decreases. As fall approaches, trees reabsorb the valuable nutrients from their leaves and store them in their roots for later use. Chlorophyll, the pigment that gives leaves their green color, is one of the first molecules to be broken down for its nutrients. As that happens, we see trees turn red, orange, and gold colors during the fall.

Okay, that's the last of the impromptu science flashbacks. So what does all that have to do with letting go? I believe we, too, can experience something beautiful as we open our hearts and hands to let go. Just as with trees, a transformation happens within us as we release things we've been holding on to tightly. Orange and yellow leaves of compassion and generosity begin to be evident in our lives. Energy from this process is stored in our hearts to encourage us through the winter months. Trees know that to grow and flourish in the spring and summer, they need to let go of their leaves. Think of the trust that is involved for a tree to release the very things that have been supplying it with food. It's not like a tree can uproot itself and go to a grocery store for more food. Trees release their leaves and trust that God will provide. We can learn so much from how trees trust God's process and timing. What things are you holding on to for a sense of security? What things in your life do you need to release to God and trust Him? Autumn shows us how beautiful it is to let things go and find our security in Christ.

Embrace the reality that we cannot take anything with us when we leave this earth

We came into this world empty-handed and will leave that way as well. None of the toys, things, or prized possessions will go with us. That's why it is so important to have an accurate perspective of what really matters most in life. We spend so much time and money trying to keep up with the Joneses or trying to impress our friends and coworkers, only to have clutter accumulate. Then we have to spend more money to store our things in facilities.

When my dad passed away two years ago, he left a twelve-by-thirty-foot storage unit full of beautiful furniture and personal effects. The space was larger than some apartments. Most of his belongings had been moved there before he went to live in a facility for seniors. After Dad's funeral, my sister, mom, and I spent three days going through all his stuff. We shared memories and shed tears as we sorted through the many items he had enjoyed during his lifetime. There was his immaculate furniture, artifacts from Uganda and from the many other countries he had traveled to over the years. There were lots of books, those he had read and a few he had written. There were lots of pictures of us in Minnesota and California. The many boxes were full of things encompassing seventy-one years of life. He took nothing with him when he went to heaven.

I want to emphasize that I'm not saying there's anything wrong with having things. Ecclesiastes 5:19 clearly states, "When God gives someone wealth and possessions, and the ability to enjoy them, to accept their lot and be happy in their toil—this is a gift of God" (NIV). Just as parents love watching their kids open and enjoy presents at Christmas or on their birthdays, God also delights in us enjoying what He has entrusted to us. The important thing is to not become consumed with them but rather put them on an altar. Before my dad moved into a senior living facility, he invited each of our immediate family to his house and asked us what items we would like to have. One sister took the piano, another sibling took his tools, another took his books, and so forth. As we embrace a realistic perspective that we do not take anything with us, it will help us facilitate the process of letting go.

Ask the Lord to show you things you need to let go of

For as long as I can remember, I've always enjoyed shopping. Whether it is in a mall, an outlet, a fun boutique, or online, I love finding new clothes and shoes. I love discovering a unique find or a "start the car" sale. Have you ever had one of those moments? You know, like the IKEA commercial from a few years back when the woman got such an incredible deal, she rushed out of the store yelling to her husband to start the car so they could get away before the managers discovered what a steal she had gotten. We all love such moments. In my early twenties, I loved shopping for a steal. I could not pass by a store that had a SALE sign in front. I remember driving out to the Palm Springs outlets for Black Friday one year. There was a long line of cars waiting to exit the freeway, and I waited for over two and a half hours just to get off the freeway that led to the parking lot. Two and a half hours!

What was I thinking? I can't even tell you what I bought that was so important. I realized then that I had let shopping consume me, and something needed to change. After some thought, I decided to go on a fast. As part of my spiritual growth, I had, at different points of my life, abstained from certain foods and observed a fast to draw near to God. But this particular year, I decided to fast from shopping... for one year. For twelve months, I did not buy any clothes, shoes, or accessories. It wasn't easy but was exactly what I needed to get my head on straight. Now, I can walk past stores that say SALE, CLOSING SALE, or even EVERYTHING MUST GO. I do not need to click on SALE, JUST DROPPED, or NEW ARRIVALS online.

What about you? Is there something that comes to mind? Anything that consumes your time, energy, thoughts, or emotions? Nothing will go into eternity with you. Ask the Lord to show you what you need to let go of. It's time to let it go!

Ask the Lord whom He would like you to bless

The Lord is constantly looking for people He can use to be a blessing to others. The thing you are holding on to may be the answer to someone's prayers. There is no greater joy than to be the person God uses to fulfill someone else's prayer request.

Several years ago, I was having a hard time being single as the holidays approached. I didn't have a husband or kids to buy presents for and was getting increasingly depressed as I looked at the empty space under my Christmas tree. As I thought about what I would buy if I was married with kids, my thoughts drifted to the families in the church who were struggling financially; the women who had a husband and kids, but no money to buy presents. I figured they would also be experiencing some level of heartache. *Maybe I can help and bring a little holiday cheer*, I thought. *What if I make it possible for someone who has a family but no money to buy presents? Perhaps I can take the cash I would've spent on gifts and give it to a family so they can get Christmas gifts for their kids.*

I had no idea how much kids' toys were, but I figured $500 would be a place to start. There were several families that came to mind as I prayed about who to give the money to. However, one family stood out. They were a blended family with eight kids ranging from a toddler to a nineteen-year-old. Even with busy schedules, the parents somehow still found the time to serve as greeters at church. Anytime I felt too tired to serve, I thought about this family, and I had no excuse. They gave so selflessly of their time regardless of their circumstances. I remember writing out the check and thinking, "God, I sure hope I'm hearing you correctly." While I had given larger checks to the church, I'd never given this amount to people I did not know that well. That weekend, I waited until they were done serving and approached them.

"Hey, Joe and Mary [names changed]. How are you guys doing? Are you ready for Christmas?" They looked at each other and then back at me. "We're getting there," Joe said. Still trying to make sure I'd heard from God, I asked, "Are you done with your Christmas shopping for the kids?" It was a week out from Christmas, and I figured they had already bought some gifts. "Actually, we haven't started," Mary said sheepishly. "I don't get paid for a few more days," Joe explained. The moment he said that, I knew the check was for them.

"The Lord put you on my heart," I said. "I don't have a family of my own to shop for and I would love to help provide Christmas for your family." When I handed them the check, their eyes got really big as they looked at each other and then back at me. With tears in their eyes, they shared, "We didn't know how we were going to be able to buy gifts for our kids. We barely have enough to cover the bills. This is going to help a lot. Thank you so much!" By that time, we were all in tears.

I've found there's no greater joy than partnering with God in blessing others. It's an incredible honor to be a vessel He chooses to use. I believe He's always listening to our prayers and looking for people whom He can answer them through. Your obedience to let go and bless someone may be the answer to their prayers.

Release gracefully without regrets

Just as trees release their leaves before winter without a fight, we also want to peacefully let things go. There is not a single tree that belabors over the fact that something that was so connected and vital to them is leaving. They know that the leaves served their purpose while attached to the tree, and as they fall to the ground, the leaves will be continuing in their purpose. The tree can release gracefully without regrets because it knows the falling leaves are setting up the tree to thrive in its next season. The tree will be able to grow and welcome new things because it released its leaves. Likewise, letting go also sets us up for the next season in our lives. Letting go puts us in the position to be ready to receive. Our hands are not full of what we are holding on to. Rather, as we live openhanded, we open ourselves up and make ourselves available to new things.

There is so much we can take away from this process, starting with embracing the fact that seasons change. It's part of life, a natural process God implemented as part of creation. We need to recognize when the season is about to change and begin to prepare for it. Deciduous trees do not wait until winter to get rid of their leaves. They begin creating cells that will let go of their leaves long before it happens. We also must not wait until winter seasons in life force us to let go. Rather, we can follow the example of trees and release things gracefully. I've never seen a tree trying to collect back the leaves it let go. It lets go and moves on. It releases and continues to prepare for the upcoming season.

I went through a similar process in my early thirties. I wish I could say I gracefully let go, but I looked more like a tree that was tugging on its leaves, afraid of what would happen after releasing them. My church was having a building campaign during which we were encouraged to pray and ask God what He would like us to give toward building His house. As I prayed, I felt like the Lord was putting on my heart to give the money I had saved as a down payment for a home. I rejected the thought at first. *There is no way God wants me to give that money away! He, more than anyone, knows how much I have sacrificed and gone without in order to save $20,000. It represents years of living not just within my means, but well below my means!*

While I wanted to help build God's house, I didn't see why I had to give away all of what I'd saved. A portion of it seemed to be more than enough. Especially from a single girl in full-time ministry. It's not like I had a nest egg or some rich relative to rely on. I was so irritated. Why couldn't God ask some rich person, who had the money to spare, to give the $20,000? *Why me?* I couldn't bear the thought of starting over to save for a down payment. It meant I wasn't going to get my own place anytime soon. I was going to have to continue living with my parents in order to save money; to continue not eating out or going shopping; and basically "not have a life" as I started to save all over again. However, as much as I tried, I couldn't shake the thought. I knew if God was calling me to honor His house above my own, He would provide the money and the house when the time came. So I wrote the check and took it to the church office.

I tried to hold my hand steady as I slowly gave the check to the finance director. My heart was beating rapidly and I felt a little light-headed as I uttered the words that it was for the church building campaign. As she received the check, there was no way she could know the significance of what she held in her hands. In a few moments, she would deposit what seemed like just another check in her daily routine, but in reality, it was the savings for my dream. It would take her less than a minute to record what took me years to collect. As she held the check in her hands, a million thoughts ran through my mind. *Did I really just give the church that check? What was I thinking? I can't afford to do that! It's too embarrassing to ask for it back, especially since I'm on staff. God, why are you having me do this? I thought you were going to answer my prayer of having a place of my own. How is that ever going to happen now?*

I'm not sure what happened for the rest of the day. Part of me felt like I had made the most foolish decision in my life, and the other part was proud of myself for being obedient to what God had called me to do and passing what I perceived was a test. I was grateful the Lord had entrusted me with the money to be able to give. But there was still a part of me that wondered if I'd really heard God correctly since it just didn't make sense financially to give all the money I had painstakingly saved to buy my first home.

What I didn't realize until years later was that the Lord was protecting me. Because I did not have the money for a down payment, I did not buy a home in the years before the market crash in 2008. Instead, I was able to buy my home at a deep discount in 2011. Even more remarkable was that in just seven years, my home appraised for over $200,000 more than when I bought it. It's like the Lord said, *Trust Me with your $20,000 to build My house and see what I can do.* He added another zero to my $20,000 and multiplied it to $200,000! Only God! This leads me to my last point.

Trust that God will take care of you and provide for your needs

I have experienced His provision so many times throughout my life that this section could be a separate chapter or even a book. One of the most significant of these moments happened in my first semester of college. For many, it is the first time to live on your own and pay bills. While my parents covered what they could, I supplemented the difference with scholarships, grants, and loans. What I did not realize was that there is a window of several weeks between when school starts and the loans go through. I quickly ran out of money while waiting for the funds to arrive. I woke up early one morning and realized I did not have any money for food. I was so stressed and didn't know what to do, so I went on a walk and cried out to God for help. I ended up at a rose garden a few miles away from campus. The sun was just coming up and highlighted the dew glistening on the grass and the rose petals. The only sound in the deserted garden was the crunching my feet made with each step on the gravel path. As I continued prayer walking, I suddenly saw a crisp $20 bill on the ground in front of me. It was completely dry! Everything else around it from the gravel to the grass and park benches was still wet from the morning dew. I looked around the garden to see if someone had dropped it, but there was no one else there. I stooped down, picked up the $20 bill, and ran my fingers on both sides of the green paper. There was not a single crease or sign of moisture anywhere on the bill. It was a miracle! Tears filled my eyes as I realized how attentive the Lord was to provide for my need. Although I could not see Him with my natural eyes, I knew that He was with me. While a $20 bill may not seem like much these days, for a college student with no money, it was like I had just won the lottery. And although it happened over twenty-five years ago, it marked me for life. That was when I first came to know Him as Jehovah Jireh, my provider.

The unknown and unexpected seasons in life provide opportunities to grow in our faith and draw closer to God. We get to know Him in a deeper way. It is often in times of great need, when we have nowhere else to go, no one else to turn to, and nothing more that can be done, that we turn to Him for help. There is something special that happens when you truly experience the Lord as your provider. There is a greater intimacy with Him, a stronger trust that develops, and a sense of peace that cannot be shaken. Like a tree, you are growing deeper roots in your faith. You walk more confidently in your calling and purpose because you know that He is the one who will open doors, make a way, and provide for your every need. He becomes the first one you turn to instead of your last resort. You no longer are driven by the need to strive and make things happen. You no longer solely rely on your own gifts, strengths, and talents. And while He will use all of that, it will be for *His* glory.

The first time God revealed himself as *Jehovah Jireh*—the Lord will provide—in Scripture was at an altar. The Lord provided a ram for Abraham to sacrifice, instead of his son. Just as He did then, God continues to provide. And just as it was then, the altar continues to be a place to encounter God in a deeper way. There is something powerful that happens when we release and let go of things as the Lord leads us to. Just like trees, we can trust that the shedding of leaves is not the final chapter. There is more to come. And while it does not happen overnight, spring and summer eventually come.

I experienced an increased intimacy with the Lord through my encounter at the altar with all my household belongings. Instead of rushing out to purchase items, I trusted Him to provide for what I needed. I knew that releasing things according to His leading was not going to lead me to harm. I had a confidence that just as He had miraculously provided the $20 bill in the rose garden so many years prior, He would continue to provide. That gave me peace. I developed a deeper sense of gratitude for the few items I had as I continued to live in my home that was not packed with things. I learned how to be content with what I had instead of continually looking for more. I was happily living my best life when I met Phil about a year and a half later. About a year after we got married, we bought a home more beautiful than anything I would have imagined and furnished with items of greater value and quality than I'd had in my meager home. I truly believe the Lord honored that posture of living openhanded and surrendering the "things" from my home on the altar. And just as I was grateful and content with what the Lord entrusted me with then, I am grateful and content with what He has entrusted us with now. As we steward them to the best of our ability, we recognize it all came from Him and belongs to Him.

My friend, you can never outgive God. He is the one who took two fish and five loaves of bread, fed over five thousand people, and still had twelve baskets left over. He is the God who kept filling the widow's jars with oil. The young boy gave the fish and bread that he had, and the Lord multiplied it. The woman gave the little oil she had left, and the Lord multiplied it. They experienced a miracle as they let go of what they had and gave it to God. He is a God who is able to multiply what we give him. Trees are only able to have new leaves grow in the spring because they let go of the old ones in the fall. It's important to note that trees don't wait until the leaves are dead in order to release them. They start the process of letting go while the leaves are vibrant and healthy. What about you? What are you holding on to more than Christ? Is there something you are being prompted to let go of? Perhaps it's a relationship that is not God's best for you, or something else you need to release. Perhaps you are robbing God of the tithe that belongs to Him. I hope the stories I shared in this chapter have shown the beauty of letting go and the fact that we cannot take anything with us when we leave this earth. I hope that you have been prompted to ask the Lord to show you things you need to let go of and whom He would like to bless through you. As you walk through that process, I pray that you will be able to release things gracefully without regrets. That you will let go of whatever He is calling you to and begin to prepare for the new thing God has for you.

The purpose of the fall season of life is to let go of things that have a hold on us or are distracting us from growing closer to Christ and becoming more like Him. I encourage you to release whatever may be preventing that. I reassure you that the "leaves" you let go of will turn into topsoil and provide nutrients to sustain you during the winter season. Continue to focus on growing and developing deep roots. Absorb the rich minerals from God's Word that will strengthen and sustain you. Because you let go of "leaves" during the fall season, you will be able to stand firm, like a tree during the winter, ready for the new growth coming in the spring season of your life.

PART 2

WINTER

unearthed from my journals:

7/24/05

Dear Lord, my whole being hurts. I could barely make it through the services today. I spent the 12 pm hour in my office silently crying. In between services, I put on a "happy" mask as I walked around greeting people and smiling while inside I was crying. The women at church commented on how beautiful I looked today. Like an "angel" in all white. I wanted to scream. I don't want to dress up anymore. It pains me to hear those comments when all I want is to hear it from a man who is passionately in love with me. I really don't feel like being at church and seeing all the couples and families. I tried to sleep away the pain today. Lord, I am hurting so bad. Where are You? You said You would never leave me or forsake me, but I feel so alone. How long must this agony continue?

6/23/16

God it's so unfair! I'm just so angry. I'm doing Your will, but You seem to have forgotten about me. My job involves connecting people with others and every day I see how people are enjoying their newfound friendships and relationships. All I want is just one connection, just ONE, Lord. How difficult can it be to bring my husband? I've prayed, I've fasted, I've walked by faith, I've thanked You in advance, I've been open to going to new places and meeting new people. I don't know what else there is left to do. We've been talking about this on and off for over 20 years! Really, Lord?!? Really? Is that what it means to give us the desires of our hearts? That we need to beg and plead for over 2 decades? I would've done things my way and been married a long time ago. But instead, I chose to follow Your ways. But look where it has gotten me. 41 years old and still single. I don't even know how to talk to You about it anymore. I just feel really hurt like You have really let me down. I feel like You are withholding from me in so many ways. I just don't know why You would sit by while I experience such heartache and loneliness. I just don't know what father would sit by while their daughter's heart breaks. Usually, dads are rushing in to save their daughters. Why are You just standing by as I sit here all alone, crying myself to sleep at night. Is this really the abundant life that You meant for me to live? I just don't feel like stirring up hope anymore. I just can't take a third decade of this madness.

8/13/19—on an airplane 2 months after my dad died

It used to be I could just jump on a plane to visit you. It used to be I could run into your arms and everything would be okay. But there is no flight to where you are. Only an endless sea of clouds. Memories play like videos against the backdrop of a clear blue sky. My continual stream of tears seems more than the ocean below. Oh, Dad, how I long to be with you. I would give anything to see your smile and the twinkle in your eye. To hear you say "I love you and I'm so proud of you." To place my head on your shoulders and feel your arms wrap around me. I miss you so much, Dad. The ache in my heart is unbearable.

    It used to be I could just pick up the phone and hear your voice. But there is no cell service where you are. I hear echoes of your voice as I go throughout the day. The lessons you taught me as a young girl now guide the decisions I make as a grown woman. There was still so much to learn from you. Still so many milestones to celebrate together. I never know what will trigger the slightest memory and release a flood of tears. I started crying at Trader Joe's as I was selecting mangoes and bananas just as you taught me. I cry every Sunday at church during worship because it's in those moments I feel close to you and that we are once again doing something together. I know we are both worshipping the Lord. Only you are in His presence with the angels beholding His glory. As much as I miss you, I know you are where we were all created to be.

CHAPTER 4

Steering Through
Black Ice

My journal echoes with the raw, unfiltered cry of the winter season. The many desperate cries out to God from the depths of a grieving heart and the frustration of when heaven is silent. "God, why are You allowing this to happen to me? Have You forgotten me? How am I ever going to make it through this painful season? If You created the world in six days, why is it taking so long for You to answer my prayer?" Some winter seasons originate from a sudden tragedy such as the loss of a loved one, a miscarriage, an affair, a drug overdose, a suicide, or the discovery of a terminal illness. Others are due to a prolonged season of waiting, trying to muster up hope, only to have dreams dashed again and again. It's the unsuccessful fertility treatments, the dates that don't lead anywhere, the medical treatments that are not working, the friends that leave you, or the toxic environment at work. The question is, how do we make it through a season that seems to have no end? How do you keep hope alive when nothing is changing and you feel stuck while everyone else's life moves on? How do you keep living when all you want to do is hibernate until winter passes?

My family and I lived in Minnesota for just over ten years. I'm convinced you have not fully experienced cold until you've been in cities such as Saint Paul and Duluth in the dead of winter. This is a state that experienced a record low temperature of –60 degrees F on February 2, 1996. Despite average winter temperatures below freezing, people in Minnesota continue to live their lives. They are not deterred by the windchill that pierces the core of every bone, the snow that continually needs to be shoveled, the car windshields that need to be scraped, or the ice that can wipe you out before you know what's happening. And ice doesn't just pose a threat to humans; it can cause damage to the natural world as well. Water that was once used (in its liquid form) to nourish a tree is now able to cause considerable damage in its solid form. Ice can accumulate on tree branches and cause them to break, or it can stress the tree and cause it to die. Just like pipes in a home, it's important that a tree's pipes do not have water in them that can freeze. This is why trees slowly dehydrate at the cellular level before the winter storms arrive in order to avoid having too much water inside when the temperature drops.

Frozen water is fascinating, when you think about it. Raindrops that freeze are called hail. Sleet is a mixture of rain and hail. Frost is water vapor that forms into little bits of ice. A snowflake is a cluster of ice crystals that fall from a cloud. Glaciers are made of snow that accumulates over many years, forming ice under the surface. Crushed ice is used to make slushie drinks for kids. My personal favorite is the mixture of frozen water with sugar and fat, otherwise known as ice cream!

Those who live in states that have real winter will be familiar with black ice. The National Weather Service defines black ice as "patchy ice on roadways or other transportation surfaces that cannot easily be seen." Because it is a thin sheet of ice, it is highly transparent and difficult to see, unlike snow or slush. It is called black ice because all you see through the clear ice is the black road surface underneath. For those who have never lived in a winter climate and experienced the panic from getting caught on black ice, allow me to explain. Imagine driving your car along the road when suddenly you lose control as it slides across the street toward another car or a snow embankment. You swore there wasn't anything on the road, but unbeknownst to you, you drove over an invisible film of black ice. Your first reaction, besides screaming for your life, is to slam on the brakes. But any experienced winter weather driver knows that's the worst thing to do! Slamming on the brakes will lock up your tires and send the car into a skid. And if you attempt to turn your steering wheel in the opposite direction, your car could end up sliding out of control. Basically, everything that would normally seem like a logical reaction is exactly what you do not want to do. Instead, you want to ease your foot off the gas and steer into the skid. It is completely counterintuitive, and like you are surrendering to the chaos, but it works. Once the car straightens out, you can stop steering into the slide. Just as there are specific things you need to know to drive through black ice, there are things we can do to steer through seasons when our lives seem to be spiraling out of control and not headed in the direction we planned.

Often, when people are waiting for something to happen, they slam on the brakes in other areas of their lives. "I'll do [fill in the blank] when I get married, when I get my degree, when I buy a home, when I have kids, when I retire, etc." As I watched friends put their lives on hold and go through a roller coaster of emotions as they waited to get married or have kids, I decided I didn't want to do that. If I was going to wait, I was determined to live my best life while doing so. I was not going to wait for a man in order to live a life of fun, adventure, purpose, and fulfillment. I was not going to slam on the brakes of my life. Over the course of two decades, I traveled the world, earned my master's degree, bought my own home, dabbled in real estate investing, ran several marathons, completed a sprint triathlon, attended leadership seminars, and took numerous culinary, fitness, golf, and dance lessons. There was no need for a bucket list because I was living it!

In addition to being intentional about living life to the fullest, there are a couple things I found to be helpful during my extended season of waiting. The first was triggered by yet another wedding invitation. And the second came out of looking for ways to sow seeds into what I was believing for. More on that in a bit.

A friend of mine came from a wealthy family, and when she got engaged, no expense was spared to create her dream wedding. The blank check went from $50,000 "budget" to over $75,000. While I was excited for her, I have to admit I was a little jealous. As much as my parents worked to provide for me, I knew they would not be able to give me such a lavish wedding. As the oldest of five siblings, I figured I would be covering the majority of the bill. This meant that the wedding of my dreams was dependent on my ability to save as much money as possible on my minister's salary. Not only did my friend have more resources than me, but she was also younger than me and had not had to wait long to get married. The months leading up to her wedding consisted of a crazy cycle of jealousy followed by guilt for feeling that way and then irritation that nothing was changing in my situation and then jealousy again for the fact that she was getting everything she wanted. With my emotions all over the place, I had so many questions for God. Again, there were no answers. The wedding day came and I slapped a smile on my face and focused on trying to have a good attitude. Afterward, I went home, still wondering why the Lord was not providing any comfort or encouragement.

A couple years later my friend shared that she was getting divorced. While I would not wish that on anyone, it taught me something that changed my entire perspective on weddings and marriage.

The majority of people spend all their time planning and preparing for a wedding, which only lasts about five *hours*, but very few people spend time preparing for their marriage, which hopefully lasts five *decades* or more. I realized we spend so much time envisioning what kind of wedding we will have: large or small, elegant or rustic, live music or DJ, ocean view, destination wedding, etc. We have our Pinterest board designed and are just waiting for a groom to complete the picture. Nothing wrong with that; I had a Pinterest board, too. However, in my winter season of waiting, instead of just focusing on a vision for my wedding day, I began to shift toward creating a vision for my marriage. I wanted to prepare for a marriage that did not fizzle out in a few years, but lasted the test of time. I began to think about what it would require to have a healthy, life-long covenant relationship. I devoured every book I could find on the subject and talked with couples from my church who had been together for many years and had a great marriage. I asked them about what had helped them develop a flourishing relationship, how they overcame challenges that they faced, what they would tell newlyweds, what investments they continue to make into their relationship and more.

As I reflected on my conversations with the couples and the wisdom they shared, I realized marriage takes a lot of intentional work. I wondered if there was anything I could do ahead of time to prepare for that. I knew I wanted to have a vibrant, healthy, fun, committed, and flourishing marriage. A lifelong Christ-centered relationship filled with grace, unconditional love, and undying respect. A union that, while not perfect, was a reflection of what God created marriage to be. I wanted a marriage that would flourish mentally, emotionally, physically, spiritually, and financially. And I knew in order for that to happen, I had a part to play. Fifty percent of that vision for marriage involved me. I spent some time thinking through what I might do to grow and learn how to flourish in those areas. Working through this is what helped me take integral steps toward walking in my purpose during unknown and unexpected seasons. While the following examples illustrate how I applied this to my future marriage, the principles apply to the many things we all face in life. As you read through the following pages, think about what you are believing for or the situation you are facing and how you can utilize the principles.

Flourish in your mind

Our minds give us the ability to think, learn, communicate, and reason. In your mind, you determine how you see the world, where you will go, what you will do, and who you will become. The Word of God gives us wisdom regarding this vital organ. Isaiah 26:3 gives us a promise of peace as we look to the Lord: "You will keep perfectly peaceful the one whose mind remains focused on you" (ISV). Romans 8:6 instructs us that "To set the mind on the flesh is death, but to set the mind on the Spirit is life and peace" (RSV). When it came to how I was thinking about the winter season of my life, my mind was skidding on black ice. I was making sweeping generalizations about things, imagining the worst possible outcomes, and jumping to negative conclusions. I couldn't see how anything was going to change. The thoughts I had regarding my prolonged season of singleness were taking me down an unhealthy path. They were bleeding into areas of my life and impacting what I was saying and doing. I knew that in order to walk in my purpose and flourish, something needed to change.

I didn't want to continue to think thoughts that were negative, defeated, hopeless, and bitter. I recognized they weren't helping anything. And it definitely was not how God was thinking and speaking about my life. Romans 12:2 encourages us, "Don't copy the behavior and customs of this world, but let God transform you into a new person by changing the way you think. Then you will learn to know God's will for you, which is good and pleasing and perfect" (NLT). So I asked the Lord to help me change how I was thinking and give me a different perspective. I asked God for His perspective. I wanted to know how He viewed this season. I wanted to align my thoughts and words with His perspective.

After I prayed, I opened my Bible to listen for what He might say through His Word. I was looking for a couple things. First, I wanted to know if any of the Bible characters had gone through a similar experience and how they had handled it. I wanted to learn from what they did right and avoid the mistakes they made. As I thought about where to start reading, I figured it would be helpful to look for any stories of other single women in the Bible and see how they met their husbands. I spent some time reading the book of Ruth and the story of Rebekah and Isaac. I found encouragement in how Ruth's humility and obedience led to her meeting Boaz. After the deaths of their husbands, Naomi urged her two daughters-in-law to return to their families. Ruth instead chose to stay with her mother-in-law, Naomi, who was also a widow. Ruth put aside her own personal interests and passionately told Naomi, "Don't urge me to leave you or to turn back from you. Where you go I will go, and where you stay I will stay. Your people will be my people and your God my God. Where you die I will die, and there I will be buried. May the LORD deal with me, be it ever so severely, if even death separates you and me" (Ruth 1:16–17 NIV). Together they returned to Naomi's hometown of Bethlehem. Once there, Ruth set out to find food for the two of them and ended up harvesting in the field of the man who became her husband.

Like Ruth, it was also through serving others that Rebekah met her future husband. According to Genesis 24, she was simply going about her routine for the day and drawing water from a well for her household. While she was at the spring, a stranger asked her for water. She not only gave him water but drew water for his ten camels. That was no small task—camels drink a lot of water! But God was doing something in the midst of what I imagine was a very tedious and laborious chore. She did not realize that she was serving Abraham's chief servant as she gave him water. He had been sent by Abraham to find a wife for his son Isaac. The servant had traveled back to Abraham's home country and stopped by a well for water. Rebekah did not know as she drew water for the stranger and his camels that she was essentially drawing water for the camels that would lead to her blessing. I love how the very camels that she watered in serving a stranger were the same camels that, only hours later, she would ride to meet her future husband, Isaac! My friend, that is how God works!

As single women, both Ruth and Rebekah focused on others and serving them. They were not desperately trying to meet someone and make something happen. Neither woman was whining about the situation or circumstances they were in. They just focused on walking in their purpose each day. They were serving, working, living their life, and going about their business. And that's what I want you and me to do. I'm grateful for all we can learn from Ruth, Rebekah, and numerous others in the Bible. Although it was written long ago, the Word of God is full of people who have walked through many of the situations we face today. You can find stories of people who had challenges getting pregnant, others who were sick and needed healing in their body, some who did not have money, others who were betrayed, abused, overlooked, cheated on, insecure, and unsure about the future. As we navigate unknown and unexpected seasons in life, the Bible is a great resource to gain wisdom from how the men and women lived their lives and responded to their situations.

After looking for Bible characters who had gone through a similar experience of being single, the second thing I looked for were any verses that applied to what I was going through. Specifically, any truths or promises I could hold on to. One of the verses that transformed how I thought and spoke about the season I was in was Proverbs 18:21: "The tongue has the power of life and death" (NIV). The words we articulate from our heart and mind have immense power. Like seeds that are planted into the ground, they will begin to grow and produce fruit. The way I was thinking at the time would have resulted in some very bizarre-looking and bitter-tasting fruit. If I continued speaking the way I was, it was going to cause me to wither instead of flourish. I knew I had some work to do. I took out my journal and began to think through and write down the negative thoughts I had about the season I was in. That took some time—there were a lot! I then pictured Jesus sitting with me and what He would say. I wrote down what I believed He would say and then how I was going to change my thoughts based on that. Here are a couple transformations I made:

Instead of thinking and saying: *Why is it taking so long for You to answer my prayer?*

I believe the Lord would say: My daughter, I love you so much. I have not forgotten you. You are everything to Me. I know when you sit and when you rise. I know the number of hairs on your head. You and I go way back. I knew you long before I knit you together in your mother's womb. Before a word is on your tongue, I know what you are thinking. I am enamored by you. I have a special song just for you. I cherish you deeply and long for you to be with Me. My loved one, you can trust Me with this desire. You can trust Me with this need. You can trust Me with this situation. I am right here with you in this season. I am working in ways that you cannot see. Receive My peace. Receive My joy. Be content in Me. Know that I began a good work in you and will bring it to completion.

I changed my thoughts and words to: *God's got this. He is working. I trust Him and His timing.*

Instead of thinking and saying: *God, how could You allow that to happen?*

I believe the Lord would say: My daughter, I am with you. Always have been and always will be. My heart broke as you went through that. It was not My desire for you to experience such agony. No parent wants to see their child suffer. Your pain was great. I know because I experienced it on the cross. It is there that I carried your burden. It is there that I felt your anger, guilt, shame, heartache, grief, and pain. I am not upset with you, and I do not see you any differently because of your feelings. I understand the disappointment, hurt, and anger that you feel toward Me. I know what it's like to feel abandoned and to wonder where God is or why He didn't do anything. I know because I, too, cried out to God at the point of My deepest pain on the cross, "My God, my God, why have you forsaken me?" (Matthew 27:46). Unlike most, I knew what the reason and the purpose of My pain were; however, that did not help My emotions or make the experience any easier. And while now is not the time to reveal why you went through what you did, know that it is not the end of your story. I can tell you from My experience that there is a purpose on the other side of your pain.

I changed my thoughts and words to: *I may not understand it now, but there is a reason for everything. Thank you, God, for giving me the grace I need and for bringing me through.*

Your turn!

Before continuing, take a moment to write down what you have been thinking and speaking about your current season. Does it align with God's perspective? If not, I encourage you to walk through the steps above and then write down a new perspective that aligns with the Word of God. It works well if it's something you can easily memorize. That way when those old thoughts resurface (and they will), you can cancel them by thinking and speaking out loud the new perspective. For example, if you are believing for healing in your body, there are lots of different verses you can memorize, write down on index cards, speak over yourself, and use in prayer. If you prefer to make a long statement (also effective!), it works well to print it out and put it in key places around your home or apartment. Examples would be your bathroom mirror, the refrigerator door, the inside of your front door, or anywhere else that you can easily see it and be reminded of the truth statements. In the words attributed to the poet William Wordsworth, "Your mind is a garden. Your thoughts are the seeds. The harvest can either be flowers or weeds."

Flourish emotionally

Proverbs 4:23 admonishes us, "Above all else, guard your heart, for everything you do flows from it" (NIV). What we let into our heart will impact us and all we say, think, and do. That's why it is so important to be selective in what we expose our heart to. We do not want to allow weeds to consume the soil of our heart. Rather we need to be proactive in removing any negative or unhealthy seeds that try to deposit themselves. As we consistently examine our heart and guard against seeds of offense, jealousy, bitterness, and resentment, we allow space for healthy things to grow. As we plant seeds of love, joy, peace, patience, kindness, goodness, faithfulness, gentleness, and self-control, we begin to flourish emotionally.

The vision I had for my future marriage was that we were both emotionally healthy with a joyful, positive outlook on life. A marriage with love, respect, honor, and healthy boundaries. One in which neither of us was bringing negative baggage into the relationship. And we were not waiting for someone to complete us or for life to start, but were both living passionate, purposeful lives full of adventure. Proverbs 14:30 says, "A healed heart [is] life to the flesh" (YLT). I asked the Lord to reveal areas where I needed healing and restoration. As things came to light, I did my best to work on those specific areas. I read numerous books and put myself in small groups and other safe spaces where I could work through some of the issues. I also sought wisdom from some of my mentors. Most important, I spent time in the Lord's presence and asked Him to bring healing to my heart.

One of the things that helped me to begin to flourish emotionally was by intentionally seeking testimonies from others who had gone through a season similar to mine and were now on the other side of it. Revelation 12:11 says, "They overcame him by the blood of the Lamb and by the word of their testimony" (NKJV). I cannot express how powerful it is to hear other people's testimonies. It stirs something within us. We start to believe, *If God could do it for them, He can do it for me, too.* If they could overcome that, there's a possibility I can overcome this, too. If God could restore and renew what the enemy meant for harm, surely He can do that for me, too. Testimonies of God's faithfulness are like medicine for our soul.

The thing is, you have got to be intentional in taking medicine. Proverbs 13:12 says, "Hope deferred makes the heart sick" (NIV). When my heart was sick from being single for so long, I intentionally sought out medicine by seeking stories of how other couples had gotten together. I literally thought I was going to write a book based just on that. As I got together with girlfriends and listened to how the Lord had brought their husbands, it helped strengthen my faith. It helped me keep believing that God was working even when it didn't seem like it.

Your turn!

In whatever you are facing today, I encourage you to intentionally seek out testimonies from people who have walked through a similar season and are on the other side. If you are believing for healing, seek out stories from cancer survivors. If you are believing to get pregnant, seek out testimonies from women who also struggled to get pregnant, or who had miscarriages and now have a beautiful child, whether by birth or adoption. If you don't know anyone, check out my website for the story of my friend who got pregnant with her first child at forty-five! Nothing is impossible for God! He created your body and is so much greater than any "biological clock"! Before we continue, take a moment to assess where you are emotionally regarding your situation. Then think about whatever you are believing for. What would emotional health look like in your vision? Write down what that would look, sound, and feel like. Next, think through whose story you can listen to that will stir your faith and help you begin to live into that.

Flourish financially

Our dreams and desires often cost money, and some of us end up going into debt as we try to make them a reality. With credit cards being so accessible, it's easy to develop habits that can cause us to wither financially. I wanted to make wise choices with the resources God had given me. To be on the path of flourishing financially before stepping into my miracle. My vision for my marriage was that it would be thriving financially with no debt, other than for real estate. I wanted to have a marriage where we saved and invested the money that we were entrusted with. I wanted us to be vessels for God to use to bless others and to be known as a generous couple.

I knew for that to happen, I needed to get some things in order. This included paying off my car, credit card, and college loans. I read financial books, took numerous classes, and attended investment seminars. I also spent time with some affluent friends and families to learn how they viewed and handled money. One investor who had made millions through real estate told me a story that I will always remember. He shared how he and his son were lying out on the beach during a family vacation. He asked his son, "What am I doing right now?" His son responded, "You are relaxing." He responded, "I'm making money." In other words, while he was lazily working on his tan, his real estate investments were making money for him. That was the first time I realized there were other ways of making money than hands-on at a job. I was determined to get my finances in order so I could step into this newfound realm of flourishing financially. Although the discipline and sacrifice were not easy, the sense of accomplishment and fulfillment was priceless. Establishing financial disciplines now will help prepare you for what God wants to entrust you with in the future.

Your turn!

There is no shortage of resources when it comes to budgeting and getting your finances in order. The challenge is in doing the work and being consistent. We know that so many of the issues that people face in life are connected to money, whether it be the lack of it or excess of it. While you are in this winter season, think about summer and what you are believing for. What would things look like financially in that season? Write them down. Then think through what steps you can take to begin to live into that now. For example, if your practice for budgeting is checking ATM slips or online accounts, how is that going to work when you have another person and their spending habits involved? Or additional mouths to feed? A team on payroll? If you are believing for a family, maybe you begin to set aside money in a new account titled FUTURE KIDS. If you are believing for a raise or a new job, a faith-stretching step would be to tithe at that new salary.

Flourish physically

Just as I wanted to flourish mentally, emotionally, and financially, I also wanted to flourish physically. My vision was that our marriage would be healthy, vibrant, and passionate physically. I wanted us to be physically active, not couch potatoes. To have a marriage in which we had a weekly Sabbath, a day that we ceased from working and rested. I recognized that just saying "I do" does not magically transform you into an active, fit, healthy person. Those habits needed to start before the wedding. A couple things I did to live into that vision included getting a personal trainer to learn how to stay in shape and taking cooking classes to learn how to cook healthy meals. I tried to learn as much as I could while I was in my winter season before spring or summer came.

Your turn!

When you envision your summer season, what does it entail physically? How will you need to exercise, eat, and rest? If you are lacking in the dedication, discipline, or desire to practice healthy habits in those areas now, it will be even more challenging to implement them when your new season comes. I encourage you to start taking small steps toward your vision. For example, if you are believing to have a family but are living on junk food and fast food, maybe learn to make a few healthy meals that would nourish your family and foster health. If you are wanting to have your own company and observing the Sabbath is a challenge for you, maybe start with a couple hours and then go to a half day. Your future employees will be so grateful to work in an environment where the owner values consistent rhythms of rest.

Flourish spiritually

Out of the five areas, this is one where I was continuously stretched during my winter season. Mainly because I really needed to lean into God in order to make it through the heartache and loneliness. I grew closer to Him through my pain and learned how to turn to Him first for everything. I knew there would be a new dynamic when I finally received the answer to my prayer. There would be another person involved. They would come with their own spiritual disciplines and relationship with the Lord. My vision for our marriage spiritually was one in which we were grounded in our faith, seeking to know Jesus more each day and become more like Him. That we both knew our identity and were walking in the purpose God had for our lives. That we knew who we were and how we lived our lives drew people to Christ.

One of the key things that came out of this process was a transformation in how I was praying. I began to pray *for* my future husband, not just *about* him. I sometimes ask my single friends, "How are you praying for your husband?" Often the response is something along the lines of, "Lord, please bring my husband, please let him be X. God, please let me get married before I turn X years old." Nothing wrong with that—it's how I prayed for many years, along with "When God, when?" and "Why is it taking so long?" However, there was a shift in my prayers when I settled in my heart that God knew who my husband was and He would bring him in His timing. Whether it was a year from now or ten years from now, I knew that it was already done. I began to thank God for my husband and to pray for him as if he were seated in front of me. I prayed for his mind, body, soul, career, spiritual growth, friends, family, work, health, finances, and our future together.*

I still continue to do that today. The only difference is that now he is actually with me as I pray! Praying with Phil came naturally. I truly believe a big part is because I had already been praying for him long before I met him. It has become a key part of our marriage and daily routine. We start each morning by praying together before we get out of bed. It has been so helpful for us to start each day by talking to God together before we talk to anyone else. It has made an incredible impact in our marriage and enabled us to flourish spiritually.

---

* To see the prayer I prayed for my husband, as well as other prayers for children, healing, etc., visit my website, gratitudewithgrace.com.

Your turn!

What do you envision your summer season will look like spiritually? For example, if you are believing to have kids, how will you teach them about God and foster their spiritual development? Are you living out the things you would want to see in your household? For example, if the spiritual disciplines are important to you, will your children see you and your spouse praying together, serving, reading the Bible, tithing, worshipping the Lord throughout the week and not just at church, thanking God, sharing your faith, etc. If they're not in practice, why not start living into that as a couple before the kids come and are absorbing everything you do...or don't do.

⚜

We started the chapter talking about the experience of steering through black ice. When the car begins to skid out of control, the natural tendency for inexperienced drivers is to slam on the brakes; but that is actually the opposite of what you should do. In the same way, when we are going through a winter season in our lives, there is a temptation to put our life on hold. I avoided that path by creating and living into a vision for what I was believing for (my marriage) and focusing on five areas to live into that. I was determined not to slam on the brakes and stop living my life while going through struggles.

Another primary way that I steered through the black ice of my winter season was by focusing on others around me instead of myself. Specifically, by looking for ways to encourage and uplift people in the circumstances they were facing. This is what kept me from isolating myself and retreating into a cave of depression. It breathed life into me as I served others in a way that put a smile on their face, brightened their day, or made them feel special. So many wonderful memories I've experienced over the years have come from blessing others. Some of the things I did were based around holidays, some around milestones, and others were just because. Below are a few of the things I did over two decades. I have an extended list on my website and would love to have you share your ideas and what you have done. Here are some ideas to get you started:

Valentines

Send gift cards to couples for Valentine's Day.

One year, I decided I was not going to focus on the fact that I did not have someone in my life to celebrate Valentine's Day. I wanted to do something different that would get the focus off myself and onto others. I decided to sow a seed into relationships I believed were healthy and flourishing. Marriages that modeled what I wanted mine to look like one day. I believe in the Biblical principle of sowing and reaping. We see that in Isaac's life, when he "planted his crops that year, he harvested a hundred times more grain than he planted, for the LORD blessed him" (Genesis 26:12 NLT). I love the promises that "one person gives freely, yet gains even more" (Proverbs 11:24 NIV), and "a generous person will prosper" (Proverbs 11:25 NIV).

I thought about where I would go with my future husband to celebrate Valentine's Day. At the time it was Fleming's Steakhouse. My order was always a medium-rare filet mignon, mashed potatoes, broccoli, and the chocolate molten lava cake for dessert. My mouth is watering already! I used my bonus check for the year to buy ten $50 gift cards to Fleming's. I printed an anonymous note that said, *Your marriage is an inspiration to me. Happy Valentine's Day*, and mailed a card and a note to each of the couples. I used my work address, which was the church, as the return address to keep things totally anonymous. Until now, I never mentioned it to anyone. It was fun to hear several of them mention in passing that they were going to Fleming's or that they had received an anonymous gift.

Single girls' Valentine's night, aka Galentine's

I hosted one of these almost every year I was single. I always wanted to create a fun and uplifting place for my single girlfriends to come together and celebrate life. Sometimes we played games, other times we just talked, sometimes we prayed for each other, and one year I arranged for a masseuse to come and give us massages. But regardless what was happening, we always had great food! One year I passed around sheets of paper with each woman's name at the top of one sheet. We then wrote down things that we appreciated about each person. When we'd finished, each of the girlfriends enjoyed reading the full sheet of beautiful things that had been written about them. When it was a smaller group gathered, I would pick one person in the room, and have everyone else acknowledge or say something they really appreciated about her. After everyone had shared, she would select the next person, and we would do the same thing for each single girlfriend. By the end of the evening, everyone left feeling incredibly loved, valued, and special.

Babysat kids for a day (for free) so parents could have a date day

I wish you could have heard the responses of the handful of parents I told, "I would like to babysit your kids for the day, *for free*, so the two of you can have a date day. I'm also happy to run any errands you need done while you are away." I got everything from, "You are going to watch all three of our kids for the entire day for *free*? We have got to pay you something!" to "We are used to leaders from the church calling because they want something from us. You don't want any-thing? You just want to bless us?" That last one pierced my heart and I made a point to impact how people experienced us as leaders going forward.

So what are some of the things the kids and I did for the day, you ask? I took them to get their favorite food—which in most cases was McDonald's. One of the couples later told me that was the highlight for their kids because their mom usually only took them through the drive-through. This time they got to actually play in the kids' area after they ate. Throughout the rest of the day, I played games with the kids, drew pictures, and cleaned their rooms. I helped them write cards for their parents and we decorated their dad and mom's bedroom with chocolate candies, candles, and rose petals. We had such a great time, and even though the kids are now young adults, they (and their parents!) still remember the day of fun.

Easter egg hunt for staff kids

I've always had a special place in my heart for the children of leaders, especially kids of church staff. Christmas and Easter are like the Superbowl for church teams. The events and services surrounding the two holidays require a *lot*, and staff kids need to be flexible in when and how they celebrate as a family. Often their parents are looking out for so many other children and adults. The kids have to learn how to share their parents with the crowd. One year, I wanted to do something special for the group of staff kids. A week before Easter, I gathered a group of single friends and we put together a private Easter Eggstravaganza for about twenty staff kids. I used the money from my bonus check to buy candy, eggs, decorations, toys, and food. We hid eggs with candy all over the church playground. We had games, food, and prizes for the kids. Staff parents got to enjoy the egg hunt and games solely with their children. They did not have to worry about any of the many things that come up when hosting an event for the community: parking, the sound system cutting out, the Easter bunny running late, the intern who bought chocolate candy that was now melting in the sweltering heat, kids who lost their parents, or parents upset about something. The staff families had a fun time and the kids left feeling so special.

Friendsgiving

I enjoyed doing numerous Friendsgiving dinners with both single and married friends because I am convinced it's healthy to be in community with both.

Angel Tree

Through Angel Tree, I had the joy of giving Christmas presents to kids on behalf of their parents, most of whom were incarcerated. Seeing the children's eyes light up in the midst of their circumstances definitely got me out of my holiday slump.

Helped friends plan anniversary celebrations

It was so discouraging for me to look on social media and realize I had friends who were already celebrating five, ten, or more years of marriage. I made a conscious decision not to have a pity party, but rather celebrate their relationship. Since I love to plan and coordinate events and surprises, I helped friends who were not as strong in that area put together a special evening for their spouse. I loved hearing from them afterward about how much they enjoyed everything.

Gave away dresses

I've already mentioned how much I enjoy shopping. When I would find a dress that was amazing and within my budget, I would buy it with the hopes of wearing it on a date with my future husband. Over the years, I had amassed quite a few fabulous dresses that still had their tags on them. One day, I was talking with a friend about her upcoming anniversary. She seemed kind of sad, and after I pressed, she shared that money was tight and she didn't have anything special to wear for their anniversary. We happened to wear the same size, so the following day, I gave her two dresses from my closet. The smile on her face and the light in her eyes were priceless. That started a tradition of giving away my clothes.

Birthdays

Sponsor a child through Compassion International and celebrate your birthdays together.

Several years ago, I was on the Bible Gateway website and was struck by a question that popped up on the screen: "Do you share a birthday with a child living in poverty?" Since birthdays have always been so special to me, this question immediately caught my attention. Normally I spend my birthdays traveling, celebrating with friends, or on some type of adventure. The thought of a child not being able to celebrate a birthday pierced my heart. I entered my birthday on the link for Compassion International and the search came up with pictures of children from around the world who all shared the same special day. I wished I could sponsor all of them and somehow have a global birthday celebration. As I browsed through the pictures and read the stories, one stood out to me. He was from Colombia and was turning three years old on the same day I was turning forty-one. I became his sponsor and together we get to celebrate our March birthdays from across the globe.

Helped a single mom plan and host her kid's birthday parties for several years

A good friend of mine is a single mom and has two kids who are now in high school and college. For the past twelve years, I have had the joy of being part of their lives as the kids grew up. Over the years I attended numerous school concerts, baseball games, and tennis matches. I've been there with their mom after the first day of school to hear about their teachers and classes and at their graduations cheering them on. We've gone to lots of movies, restaurants, and Dodgers games, and even vacationed together. One of the things I have enjoyed the most is helping my friend plan, coordinate, and host the birthday parties for her kids over the years. One year we transformed her backyard into an outdoor theater, complete with a red carpet and concession stand. Another year we transformed my house into a spa where the girls got facials and mani-pedis. Because putting on a party for a group of kids can be overwhelming for a single parent, this was something I and some of our other single friends enjoyed helping her with. We loved being a part of the kids' lives and seeing them grow up. When I got engaged, it was so special to be able to give my promise ring to my friend's daughter. For most of her life, she had seen me wear it as I waited for God and trusted Him to bring my husband.

Led a small group

I have enjoyed being part of a church small group since I was in high school. I am still friends with several of the girls from my high school and college groups. At some point along the way, I started leading groups and not just attending them. Over the years, I led groups that were focused on Bible study, leadership, and other times on fun outings, sports, and nutrition. My favorites have been when I gathered together some single girlfriends to read and discuss a book on relationships and marriage. Some favorites are *The Five Love Languages*, *The Power of a Praying Wife*, and *His Needs, Her Needs*. I also had some of the married pastors and couples in the church come and share their wisdom on relationships. I always wanted us to learn as much as possible before getting engaged and looking at the world through rose-colored lenses. If you have not led a small group before, I encourage you to look into hosting one. Getting together with people who are in a similar stage in life or believing for the same thing and providing a safe place to talk and pray for one another is priceless. That is how I kept myself from isolating in a cave of depression.

Served a healthy family for a year

During a painful time in my journey, I could feel myself becoming cynical about marriage and family. People who I thought would always be together were getting separated, including my dad and mom. If my parents, who met at church, led Bible studies, and were active in ministry could not make it, what hope was there for the rest of us? I knew I needed healing for my broken heart. I needed a new vision for relationships. I needed to observe and learn from a healthy marriage and family. However, I knew I could not just walk into a household and say, "Hey, I want to hang out and just watch you guys live your life." But I was desperate and willing to do anything to see the behind-the-scenes of a healthy family. I needed to know if it was for real or crumbling at the cracks.

I decided to enter by serving. One of the pastors at the church I was attending had five kids. I went and introduced myself to his wife and offered to help with anything she needed one day out of the week. "If you show me how you like to clean your home, I will do it for free." Surprisingly, she agreed—I think because she was pregnant with their sixth child. For just under a year, I helped her with household chores. I did not accept any payment. Instead, I got something money could not buy. I got to observe a healthy family behind the scenes. I saw how the pastor honored and loved his wife and led his family. I saw how she supported and respected him and nurtured her children. I saw how they extended grace to one another, how they loved people in the community, and lived their faith the best they knew how. Sure, they weren't perfect—no one is. But it restored my hope in the value of marriage and family.

I could easily have written several chapters on the many things I did in order to not "slam the brakes" and put my life on hold while steering through the black ice of my winter season. After all, the stretch of ice lasted for two decades! However, I hope the few things I mentioned sparked some ideas to keep your faith in the midst of whatever you are facing. I hope you are encouraged and empowered by having created a vision for your summer season and determined ways to live into that now. I hope you experience fulfillment as you intentionally focus on others in the midst of your struggle. As you continue to do that, your perspective will change and you will discover a new purpose in the unknown and unexpected seasons of life.

CHAPTER 5

Can Someone *Please* Stop This Storm?

"**I**'m sorry, we did everything we could…"

I did not recognize the phone number or the voice of the man speaking. The call was from an out-of-state area code, so I figured he must have called the wrong number.

"Mel was unresponsive…"

The stranger's words ricocheted through my cell phone like a stray bullet grazing my brain, rendering me incapable of comprehending the words that followed. Bursting through my lungs, they left me grasping for air as the bullet lodged deep in my heart, triggering it to beat faster than humanly possible.

"Wait!" I interrupted the man, who calmly identified himself as a doctor from a hospital in Minnesota. "Are you telling me my dad is *dead?*" I stammered.

I did not understand what was happening, who the stranger was, or how he was connected to my dad. I peered out the car window, looking for anything to tell me if this was for real or if I was in the middle of a really bad nightmare. People were casually going about their day, walking to and from their rental cars, unaware of the explosion that had detonated in my vehicle. I'd just landed in Los Angeles from Charlotte, North Carolina. I'd flown in to surprise my mom for Mother's Day. Dad had gone in for a simple test only a few hours ago—about the same time I'd boarded the plane for my cross-country flight. He was having a biopsy to identify what was causing some symptoms he was experiencing. It was just a test! A simple test! There was nothing complicated about it! It's not like it was a major procedure. I had just FaceTimed him last night and he was in good spirits. There was no way this could be true! And yet I heard the doctor say the same devastating words again: "I'm so sorry. We did all we could."

I tried to focus as he explained how Dad's heart did not respond once they flipped him over after the test was completed. I mustered a few follow-up questions, knowing I was going to have to tell the family and they would all be looking for answers as to why this happened. While Dad had been battling Parkinson's for several years, there was no indication today would be his last day. I hung up the phone and stared at it, knowing my next call would release a nuclear bomb in our family.

Losing a loved one, whether it be due to illness, miscarriage, malpractice, overdose, suicide, crime, or natural disaster, is undoubtedly the worst pain we experience in life. It's like a winter storm whose strong winds and cold air burst in, uprooting everything and destroying life as you had previously known it. The blizzard shows no mercy to anything it encounters. Not only are life and health susceptible, but also careers, businesses, life dreams, relationships, and anything we value. These severe storms can start suddenly. One day you go in for a medical checkup or a test and the next day you receive the results revealing a terminal illness. One day you and your spouse are celebrating your anniversary and another day you discover their infidelity. One day your son or daughter is doing great at school and the next day you get a phone call from the principal. One day you are having a great time with your friends and colleagues and the next you are stabbed in the back. One day you are employed and the next you are let go when the company downsizes. One day you are having the best quarter in your business and the next you lose your major account to a competitor or you have to close. One day the sun is shining, the sky is blue, birds are chirping, and all is at peace. The next day cold weather and strong winds assemble, releasing a blizzard of snow. The amount of snow in the air can become so great that the visibility is near zero. The resulting whiteout makes it impossible to see, although it is daylight. Winter storms create dangerous conditions because of cold temperatures, wind, snow, and ice. Exposure to such severe elements can lead to frostbite, hypothermia, and heart attacks from overexertion. Because winter storms can last from a few hours to several days, they cause increased risk of car accidents and carbon monoxide poisoning, in addition to the loss of heat, power, and communication services. The weight of snow can cause roofs to collapse and knock down trees and power lines.

Because blizzards and winter storms can be so dangerous, there's been a lot of work put into helping us prepare and make sure we are out of harm's way. Those who do not live in the northern United States may be surprised to know that warning signals are used to alert the public of impending blizzards or severe storms. These days, emergency warnings can be received through your smartphone, the internet, social media, TV, radio, and informational signs on highways. The goal is to notify people so they can prepare and seek cover. A warning that a storm is coming makes all the difference in surviving the onslaught. Unfortunately, that does not translate to our personal lives. There is no warning signal for the blizzard that blasts into your world and obliterates your heart. The sudden death of a loved one, the extreme hurt of an affair, the call from the police regarding your child, the accident, the termination, the miscarriage, the betrayal of a friend or colleague, the test results from the doctor. We do not see the storm coming until we are caught up in the midst of it. Out of nowhere, life as we've known it is no longer the same.

It's hard to prepare for something we did not see coming. None of us wake up expecting to experience an emergency of any kind. But there are some things we can do ahead of time to prepare for the winter storms that will inevitably come.

Seek safe shelter

One of the most important ways to survive a winter storm is to seek shelter. You don't want to face a snowstorm without a safe, warm place to ride it out. If you don't have safe shelter, you can get hypothermia or freeze to death.

When it comes to the storms of life, we also need to find safe shelter—a place where you can go to be protected from the elements. In this case, that shelter could be with your family, trusted friends, a counselor, or your small group.

The first time I experienced one of life's significant storms was in college. I was in my junior year, on track to complete the requirements for my major and graduate the following year. That's when 100 mph winds suddenly blasted into my world, pouring down a solid wall of snow, sleet, and ice. Hail the size of golf balls assaulted my heart as I heard that my dad and mom were getting a divorce. They had been married over twenty-two years, and while they'd had their fair share of "silent treatment" fights, nothing seemed out of the ordinary. They were always able to move forward and focus on the needs of their five kids. Being away at college for over two years, I did not see their separation coming. The sudden avalanche of snow crushed my bones. I had no strength to try and dig myself out to learn anything in class. My body slowly went numb from the below-freezing temperature. I tried to study but could not see the words on the page past the freezing rain that blinded my eyes. My grades plummeted as hypothermia set in, forcing me to switch majors and push graduation back a year. My world collapsed under the weight of the storm while everyone else's just kept on moving as if nothing had happened.

I was hurt and angry at my parents for not working things out and fighting to save their marriage. Angry that they had not kept what I thought was their side of the bargain. I felt I had kept my end of the bargain by being a great daughter. I followed their rules, I got good grades, and I stayed out of trouble. I had not given them grief growing up and had helped however I could with my younger siblings. Somehow, that created in me an unspoken expectation that they would also do likewise. I was angry because I felt let down not only by my parents but also by God. He did not answer my desperate prayers to keep my parents together. I felt so betrayed. I did not want to talk to God, hear any Scripture, or go to church. I didn't want to see anyone, talk to anyone, or be around anyone. It was all I could do to breathe.

I was in that state when my two friends found me. I honestly don't recall what, if anything, they said; but what I do remember is how they stayed with me through the roller coaster of my emotions. They held me as I cried, listened as I vented, and sat with me as I lay in a fetal position, too numb to move. I call these the 3 a.m. friends, the small handful of people you can call at any time of night and they will answer. They will meet you in the storm and sit with you until it passes. If you have experienced the depth of such pain, you know that trying to tough it out on your own does not get you very far. We need others. We need friends who will fight for us when all our strength is gone. The kind of friends we read about in Exodus 17 when an army of warriors attacked the Israelites. Moses sent Joshua to lead the Israelites in battle against the Amalekites who had invaded them.

Meanwhile, Moses, Aaron, and Hur went up to the top of a hill and Moses held up the staff of God in his hands. "As long as Moses held up his hands, the Israelites were winning, but whenever he lowered his hands, the Amalekites were winning. When Moses' hands grew tired, they took a stone and put it under him and he sat on it. Aaron and Hur held his hands up—one on one side, one on the other—so that his hands remained steady till sunset. So Joshua overcame the Amalekite army with the sword" (Exodus 17:11–13 NIV). We all need Aaron and Hur friendships in our lives. People who will come alongside us when we are too heartbroken to worship, too angry to pray, or too weary to go on. They will do what needs to be done to provide shelter for us in our vulnerable state.

Just as we need to identify shelter *before* the storm, we want to establish safe friendships before we find ourselves in the middle of life's storms. If such friendships are not currently in your life, I encourage you to be intentional about developing some now. A good way to connect with people is by joining a small group at your local church. There are plenty of opportunities to be an Aaron and a Hur to others who are currently hurting. While it would be amazing to be there for every person you know who's in pain, only God can do that. Instead, ask Him whom He would like you to reach out to. Maybe send that person a text to let them know you are thinking about them and praying for them. I like to leave voice messages with a prayer they can listen to. Send flowers or make them chocolate chip cookies. Write a note, grab coffee, or take someone to lunch. Be a friend who notices when something is off, who sees past the smile disguising their pain, who hears their silent cries for help, who leans in and asks how they are *really* doing. Create a safe space to be authentic, real, loved, and accepted. And someday, you may find refuge there in the midst of your own storm. I understand for some of you this might seem overwhelming because your work involves travel or perhaps your spouse's job requires your family to move every few years. I would still encourage you to do what you can to make the investment, because 3 a.m. friends can be from across the country. They don't need to be in your time zone; they just need to answer the phone when you call.

Stay warm

As I already mentioned, during a cold winter storm, there is a risk of frostbite, hypothermia, and a heart attack from overexertion. The signs of frostbite include numbness and loss of feeling in fingers, toes, and around the face. Hypothermia is when the body loses heat faster than it can produce. Body temperatures fall below 95 degrees, causing disorientation, memory loss, slurred speech, drowsiness, and uncontrollable shivering. To prevent such conditions, it is important to go to safe shelter and, once there, stay warm. There are some key measures you can take to keep your family and your home warm, such as wearing layers, using blankets and an electric space heater, and enjoying hot food and drinks.

In the storms of life, we also want to stay warm and avoid emotional frostbite and hypothermia. Sudden emergencies and unexpected circumstances can leave us feeling numb, exhausted, and confused. When we notice our health starting to be affected by the situation, it is important to get professional help. One such resource is a licensed therapist.

I had my first counseling session when Phil and I went through premarital sessions in preparation for our wedding. I received so much insight and value from the experience that I continued having sessions periodically afterward. Because I had been talking with my therapist about my dad's failing health for over a year, it was like he already knew him. When my dad passed away, my therapist was well aware that just like a severe winter storm, the death of my hero was going to leave massive damage. Because I did not wait until the crisis happened to seek counseling, I did not have to catch my therapist up to speed on who my dad was, what he was like, or how much he meant to me. As a result, he was able to be a vital voice of comfort and healing in my sudden storm. His compassion, wisdom, and understanding helped me not go numb in the midst of grieving and fulfilling my role as dad's executor.

Stay off the roads: Don't make major moves or decisions

During a winter storm, officials tell you to stay off the roads. There's a reason for that. Hundreds of people are injured or killed each year by exposure to cold and by vehicle accidents due to icy roads.

In the same way, during the storms of life, we want to stay off the roads by not making any major moves or decisions. Our ability for logical thinking and decision making becomes slippery when we are frozen by a tragedy.

Over the years, I've officiated a number of funerals. Some were for people I knew personally while others I only got to know when family members, with tears in their eyes, shared stories and memories of their loved one as we planned their service. Some deaths were due to sudden accidents and others were caused by prolonged illness. Whether or not they were prepared for all that is involved with the passing of a loved one, I would encourage them not to make any major life-changing decisions in the midst of their grief. Life's storms have a way of uprooting everything in our world. As things are shifting in disarray, it is not the wisest time to make big decisions and try to plant roots in an unstable environment. While there will always be some immediate decisions that need to be made in order to address the crisis, as much as possible, we want to stay off the roads until the storm passes. If you are currently in the middle of a storm and need to make some important decisions, I highly encourage you to seek counsel from trusted mentors or friends. It's not the best idea to make major changes on your own in the middle of a storm. Be intentional about talking through the options and risks of what you are considering with someone who is working on your behalf. Someone who is not in the same storm with you.

Have an emergency pack prepared

Having lived in different regions of the country where tornadoes, hurricanes, earthquakes, fires, and mudslides are prevalent, I understand it can be hard to know what you will need in a natural disaster. However, the time to put together an emergency pack is well before the storm. In life, it's not *if*, but *when* we will go through a storm, so I thought it might be helpful for us to work on putting an emergency pack together. Some of the basic things we want to include are:

A flashlight, batteries, and portable charger—God's Word

I've spent most of my life in California, so when Phil and I bought our current home in Alabama, which sits in tornado alley, I did not have a full appreciation of the fact that there was a huge generator on the property. Having now lived through a couple tornadoes and numerous rainstorms, I am very grateful for this machine that I had previously viewed as an eyesore just to the side of the house. For those like myself who are not familiar, the power often goes out in a storm, and it can be hours or days before the power company gets it back on. In the meantime, a generator kicks in and is a temporary source of power. Even with that backup, Phil and I make sure to have plenty of flashlights, batteries, and portable chargers ready to go.

In preparation for life's storms, we want to have the Word of God accessible. Psalm 119: 105 says, "Your word is a lamp to guide my feet and a light for my path" (NLT).

However, it's almost impossible to read the Bible during a

personal storm when you get the call that "it's over." Or when your phone keeps ringing with lawyers and debt collectors. Or when your cell is completely silent as you anxiously wait to hear from your teenager who hasn't come home. Or as you sit in the emergency room waiting to hear whether your parent is going to make it after their heart attack. It's in the moments when we can't even think straight that we desperately need hope and encouragement. What I've found helpful in situations where words on a page do not make sense is to have someone else do the reading. Specifically, to have an app that reads Scripture to you. There is something comforting about having another "person" speak God's truth and promises over you when you are too hurt, defeated, or discouraged to read them on your own. The time to find what app works best for you is *now*, before the storm.

Food and water—worship

It goes without saying that we need to pack several days' worth of supplies of food and water to sustain us in a natural disaster. And there are numerous things we can turn to, to sustain us in a personal storm. I look for something that is going to meet me in my pain, frustration, or anger and give me peace while helping me refocus, heal, and regain hope. I have found the most effective thing for me is listening to worship music. Note I said *listening*, because there are times the heartache is so deep, I just can't get the words out to sing them myself. I've found in such seasons that having a playlist with worship music has been the sustenance my heart needs during a storm. I'm notorious for having a song or a playlist on repeat. Phil once asked me why I don't like rewatching a movie, reading a book a second time, or returning to the same vacation spot, but I will listen to the same song all day. I explained that sometimes you just have to get the song into your spirit until it changes your outlook.

Family and emergency contact information

Any good disaster preparedness kit includes a list of important phone numbers. This includes numbers for family members near and far, police, fire, doctor, medical/home insurance information, utility company contacts, etc. They are the people we call after a snowstorm, tornado, earthquake, fire, flood, or other natural disaster. But what about life's disasters? Do you have a list of people to call if the foundation of your marriage is suddenly shaken with the discovery of a pornography addiction or an affair? Or when a tornado funnel forms as your doctor shares the results of your tests? Do you have people to call when your reputation, life's work, relationships, family, hopes, and dreams have been upended by an unexpected storm? In addition to the 3 a.m. friends we discussed previously, you need a few more people. Other phone numbers that you may want to have on your life emergency contact list include your pastor and a counselor or licensed therapist.

And I *highly* recommend having at least one friend who has been through a difficult winter season and is on the other side. While it's important to have your 3 a.m. friends who know you the best and will always be there for you, you need at least one person you can call who knows what it's like to hit rock bottom, who knows the devastation of having lost everything. Someone who knows what it's like to lie in a fetal position on the bathroom tile floor surrounded by blood, having just miscarried. Someone who knows what it's like to lie alone in a bed drenched with tears, trying to breathe, after discovering their spouse is leaving them for someone else. A friend who knows what it's like to see their life flash before their eyes as they receive the test results from the doctor. A friend who knows the unexplainable sorrow and heartache from seeing the parent who raised them lying lifeless in a hospital bed. A friend who has woken up to find their life savings gone, betrayed by a loved one or colleague. A friend who has buried their head in the clothes hanging from the closet they shared with their late spouse, trying to hold on to the scent that embraced them for so many years.

You need a friend who has been through any one of such storms and is on the other side. They don't need to have gone through the exact same crisis you are going through. You need what they learned in their storm: their ability to fight. How to breathe through the pain. How to make it through. These friends are not put off by your screams, wails, expletives, or completely numb state. They are not trying to preach to you or come up with something to say. In fact, they might not say anything at all. They may just sit with you. And if they do say something, it may just be: "I got you." All that you need to feel seen and heard and know you are not alone in your storm.

Some storms just can't be predicted

There are some winter storms that are a challenge to forecast. Freezing rain can sneak up on you, because there is very little difference in temperature between freezing rain, sleet, or snow. Another storm that is also difficult to predict is a ground blizzard. Whereas traditional blizzards consist of wind and heavy snowfall, ground blizzards occur with no snowfall. Both result in a whiteout with very low visibility, but ground blizzards result from very strong winds raking up fallen snow and blowing it around. It is hard to predict the wind's ability to pick up old snow and make it airborne. I found myself thrust in such a storm when my phone started ringing in the middle of the night. The name of an extended family member whom I had not heard from in a long time lit up the screen. I answered the phone and heard heart-wrenching wailing. Through her sobs, I was able to make out two words: "Mary's dead."

I sat up in bed and turned on the light, sure I was having a nightmare. But before I could fully register what was happening, the words came through the phone again with more anguish: "Mary is dead!"

"Nooooo!!!" I cried out. "She can't be dead. I just talked to her the other night. She was going to call me back!"

Mary had called me earlier that week around 1:00 a.m. I immediately answered, concerned that something was wrong. She had already called me twice in the past month to let me know her doctor had just told her she had Alzheimer's. As I answered the phone, I was prepared to once again respond with compassion upon hearing the news for a third time. However, once she heard my sleepy voice, she realized she had forgotten the time difference between Uganda, where she was calling from, and the Central Time Zone of the United States, where I was, and apologized profusely. She assured me she was okay and that there was no emergency. She insisted I go back to sleep and said she would call me later. My phone did ring two days later…but it was not Mary.

Phil woke up and tried to comfort me, but I was inconsolable. The ground blizzard that started in Uganda had crossed the Atlantic Ocean and swept into Birmingham, Alabama. Its winds stirred up raw emotions of shock, despair, and anger throughout the following days. Mary was like a mom to me and had helped me through so many things over the course of my forty-six years of life. She was always full of joy and brought laughter into every room she entered. Although she had been dealing with diabetes, Alzheimer's, and other health challenges, her love of life and people did not wane.

"God," I cried out, "how come You didn't give me any warning this was going to happen? Why didn't You prompt me to stay on the phone with Mary in the middle of the night if You knew she was going to die!" My despair quickly turned to anger toward God. That may sound sacrilegious, but that was the reality of where I was at. Mary was the third family member who had died in less than three years. First it was my dad, then a year later my grandma had passed, and now my aunt Mary. I felt betrayed by God. He knew this was going to happen so unexpectedly, and He did not say or do anything. I know we all eventually pass away, but Mary was only sixty-three. She still had so much life to live. I could not understand why God, having the power to heal her, did not intervene.

If I had known, I would've jumped on a plane to Uganda just so I could have one last hug, one last chance to see the sparkle in her eyes, hear her contagious laugh, and see her million-dollar smile light up the room. One last opportunity to tell her how much I loved her and how grateful I was for all she had done for me. I was so angry that God had robbed me of that opportunity. He knew how much it was going to devastate me to lose my aunt and He didn't give me any warning. Who *does* that? Who knowingly sees a friend in the path of an oncoming storm and does not try to warn them? Even strangers warn each other! Why didn't God, who knows me and loves me, warn me this was going to happen? Who wouldn't have appreciated an alert before the flash flood that washed away all your savings; the mudslide that clogged the arteries, organs, and bone marrow in your body; or the tsunami that hit your marriage and demolished your family?

For weeks I fluctuated between unstoppable tears, emotional outbursts expressing my hurt and pain to God, and giving God the silent treatment. I knew my ignoring Him was not accomplishing anything other than hurting me more, but I just didn't feel like talking to Him after He had withheld such a vital piece of information in our last conversation. Maybe you have experienced similar frustration and hurt. *God, how come You didn't give me a heads-up that my spouse was cheating on me? How come You didn't tell me this disease was attacking my internal organs? Why didn't You make me aware of what my teenager was getting into before it was too late? Why didn't You warn me that this person, this job, this team was so toxic and out to destroy me?*

One day, a good friend asked me: "What if the Lord had told you?

What if He had given you the warning you were looking for? What would you have done? We both know exactly what you would've done. You would have fervently prayed for God to spare Mary's life. And if after all that, He took her home, how would you feel?"

I exhaled sharply as I realized what she was bringing to light. I would have actually been in a worse space if what she was describing happened. Yes, I would've known what was about to occur, but it would not have prevented or alleviated the destruction of the storm.

As I continued to think about the question my friend asked me, I realized this "need to know" isn't just a Grace issue; it's a humanity issue. Our need to know goes way back to Adam and Eve. The Lord had put them in a beautiful garden, filled with birds, animals, and fruit. They could have enjoyed the peace and tranquility of this paradise, but instead they obsessed over knowing the one fruit that the Lord had said not to eat.

"And the LORD God commanded the man, 'You are free to eat from any tree in the garden; but you must not eat from the tree of the knowledge of good and evil, for when you eat from it you will certainly die'" (Genesis 2:16–17 NIV).

As we know, they both ate the fruit. And although nothing seemed different on the outside, life as they knew it was forever changed.

"Then the eyes of both of them were opened, and they realized they were naked; so they sewed fig leaves together and made coverings for themselves. Then the man and his wife heard the sound of the LORD God as he was walking in the garden in the cool of the day, and they hid from the LORD God among the trees of the garden" (Genesis 3:7–8 NIV).

The need to know is definitely a good and necessary thing in some areas. We need to know how much money is in our bank accounts in order to make wise decisions. We need to know our kids' schedules and who their friends are. We need to have regular checkups so we can know the condition of our health. It is wise to pursue the knowledge of such things.

However, there are some things that will actually cause us harm if we know about them. In Adam and Eve's case, the knowledge of good and evil impacted their relationship with God and each other. What they discovered caused them to hide from God and created an emotional and physical distance from Him. Rather than eagerly awaiting to connect with God as they had previously done, they now rushed in the opposite direction when they heard Him walking toward them in the garden. How they saw themselves and God had impacted the intimacy and innocence in their relationship, and they could not undo that.

When God called out to him and asked, "Where are you?" Adam responded, "I heard you in the garden, and I was afraid because I was naked; so I hid" (Genesis 3:9–10 NIV). Fear and shame were introduced into a space that had previously been healthy, secure, and safe. Later in the chapter we see that "the LORD God banished him from the Garden of Eden to work the ground from which he had been taken" (Genesis 3:23 NIV). Adam and Eve's desire to experience the fruit from the tree of knowledge of good and evil led to them tasting it and resulted in them losing so much of the good in their life and gaining heartache they did not know existed. Their story shows us there are some things that having knowledge of will cause us more harm than not knowing.

It was life changing when I realized I *do not* need to know everything! I don't need to know how this current situation is going to change. I don't need to know how that issue is going to be resolved overnight. I don't need to know what everyone is doing on social media. I don't need to know what people are thinking about what I said, what I did, or what I look like. I don't need to know what the cooks are doing in my favorite hole-in-the wall restaurant because I may never go back again. I definitely don't need to know what every dessert on the menu tastes like! I don't need to know when or how God is finally going to answer my prayer and give me a miracle. I just don't need to know all that. This has been so freeing as I live my life and go about my day. Now, when the curiosity or anxiety of not knowing something begins to stir, I tell myself, "I don't need to know that." However, it can be easier said than done a lot of times. In those moments, what I found to be helpful is to shift the focus from what *I think* I need to know, to what the *Word says* I should know. Psalm 46:10 says, "Be still, and know that I am God" (NIV).

We need to know Him, and specifically, that He is God. That means He knows every situation and challenge you and I are facing. He is in control. He knows what you are stressing about. Your child who is questioning their faith and doesn't want anything to do with God? He knows. Those arguments you've been having with your spouse, that issue in your marriage? He knows. The fatigue from the unexpected season we have all been through and the anxiety over the future that is unknown? God knows that, too. And because He knows, we can release our stress over the situation and let go of agonizing over a plan to resolve it. We can focus on knowing God and being with Him. As we sit with Him, we realize that there isn't a frantic air around Him, but rather peace. As we sit with Him and focus on knowing Him, a greater intimacy develops and our trust in Him increases. Sitting with Him can be in silence, worship, prayer, or just being still.

I want to encourage you to let go of that need to know everything about everything. We do not need to stay up all night worrying and trying to figure things out. Let's focus on knowing God. And the more we know Him, the more we can trust that He is in control and He is working. His plans are so much better than anything we could come up with on our own.

Be alert for hazards after a storm

It can be so tempting to get out after being stuck inside for several days because of a strong winter storm. But as you venture outside, it's important to stay alert for fallen debris, ice, potholes, and other road hazards. It is hard to anticipate the potential hazards after a personal storm, especially if it's something you have not experienced before. You do not see the emotional pothole until you have fallen into it. That is what happened to me in the months after my dad passed. I began to develop a deep, paralyzing fear. Because my dad's death was so sudden and unexpected, I feared what might happen to other family members. Because I had not been able to be there with him and for him in his final moments, I feared missing out on the final moments of other loved ones. As I grew increasingly anxious over the safety and well-being of my family members, I knew that I was walking down an unhealthy road. I had multiple conversations with Phil, our counselor, and with the Lord about this growing concern. I was not making much progress until, one day, the Lord gently corrected me by saying, "Grace, stop living in fear, your dad was ready to go." In my heartache and grief, I had not thought about what my dad might have been thinking or feeling at the time of his death. I assumed that anyone in that position would be fighting to stay here with family and friends. I suddenly realized that what was the absolute worst day of my life was actually my dad's best day. Dad had been walking with God for over fifty years. Five decades of worshiping the Lord, serving Him, and telling others about Him. This was the day he had been waiting for. After years of following him, Dad was finally able to see his Maker face-to-face.

What I came to realize is that just as Jesus was with my dad, receiving him with open arms, Jesus was also holding me and standing with me in the storm. He was there all along. It was hard to realize that in the season leading up to Dad's passing. Dad had been suffering from

Parkinson's. It was so hard to see the man who had carried me on his shoulders, taught me how to play tennis, and fostered my love for education now so frail in a wheelchair, barely able to speak. Leading up to the biopsy procedure, Dad showed signs of getting better. When I had FaceTimed him the night before, his skin was vibrant and his voice was stronger than normal. I was actually able to understand what he was saying and clearly hear him say, "I love you." I now realize that Jesus was in that final conversation, giving Dad's vocal cords the strength to express his love for me one last time.

The three-year winter storm of family deaths was a very painful part of my spiritual journey. I experienced windchills that left me barely able to breathe. But in the whiteout blizzard when I could not see my way, I experienced the Lord as *El Roi*, the God who sees me, and *Jehovah Roi*, the Lord is my Shepherd, gently guiding and sheltering me through the storm. In the flurry of my emotions, *Jehovah Shalom* gave me peace. And when I fell into the pit, *Immanuel*, God with us, met me there and let me know I was not alone. Just as the Lord was with me through the most difficult storm of my life, He is also with you. Holding you when you feel abandoned and alone. Carrying you when you feel like you can't go on. You can trust Him to bring you through the storm. I pray that whatever you are going through, you experience His presence in a way you never have before and know that you are not alone.

CHAPTER 6

Weathering Winter Windchills

Sometimes the challenge is not about surviving the sudden storm, but about weathering the consistent winter windchill. The National Weather Service defines windchill as what the air temperature feels like to the human skin owing to the combination of cold temperatures and winds blowing on exposed skin. Basically, it's how chilly you feel when you go outside and the wind blows on your face. Because of the wind, you often feel a lot colder than what the temperature actually is.

In life, a windchill sets in when the environment and relationships around you grow cold. Conversations are increasingly icy, and connection is sparse as people obsess over their need to thrive. You have a deep longing to belong, but no one seems to be interested in who you are or what is going on in your world. Alone and isolated, you know that you have so much to give and contribute, but for some reason you remain unseen and overlooked. In the winter whiteout, the world does not see the value that you bring. You wonder how much longer you can continue to survive in an environment with no warmth, very little sun, and chilling wind. With good forecasts and ample warning, you are able to steer through winter storms that have a start and an end, but it's the ongoing winter windchill that has the ability to take you out. In such situations, it helps to glean wisdom from nature's ability to survive.

When temperatures drop, we have the option to head back indoors and sit around a fire or enjoy some hot cocoa. But animals do not have such a luxury. Although it can be challenging for them to find food or shelter, they have learned several ways to adapt and weather winter windchills. Some animals put on layers and grow warm fur. Still others survive by going into hibernation. Some animals migrate to warmer areas. Migrating is how my parents and I weathered a life-threatening windchill in 1976 when I was just under two years old.

⁂

My dad and mom knelt on the hard floor of our two-bedroom flat while I slept in the adjoining room. Through the closed windows, they heard the popping sound of gunfire from the surrounding neighborhoods. Dad reached for Mom's hand as they closed their eyes in prayer.

> "He who dwells in the secret place of the Most High,
> Shall abide under the shadow of the Almighty.
> I will say of the LORD, 'He is my refuge and my fortress;
> My God, in Him I will trust.'"

Dad recited Psalm 91 from memory as Mom quietly mouthed the words with him. Each line echoed the cry of their hearts, as they turned to God for protection in the midst of grave surroundings. He continued:

"Surely He shall deliver you from the snare of the fowler
And from the perilous pestilence.
He shall cover you with His feathers,
And under His wings you shall take refuge."

Tires screeched outside. Dad abruptly stopped his prayer as his eyes locked with Mom's. They both knew the sound and what it meant. The military and the secret service were known for their high-speed driving and sudden stops. You never wanted to hear tires screech in your immediate vicinity because it could mean the soldiers were coming for you. Dad jumped up and peered out the window overlooking the small parking lot. Through the meager outdoor light, he was able to make out a military jeep and the white Peugeot 504 that had pulled up behind it. He glanced back at Mom, confirming their fear. The white vehicle was used by the State Research Bureau and was an especially unwelcome sight. Many unfortunate civilians had been imprisoned in a makeshift coffin as the trunk of a Peugeot 504 closed upon them.

Turning toward the window again, Dad watched as armed men in dark green uniforms got out of the vehicles and approached the building. With machine guns slung behind their backs, the men pounded up the stairs. Following closely behind were men dressed in blue jeans and jackets. Their clothes and sunglasses made them easily identifiable as part of the SRB. Dad reached down and took Mom by the hand. "Come," he said quietly as he helped her to her feet. He turned off the light and led her into the room where I was sleeping. They held hands as they stood beside my crib and Dad continued his prayer.

"You shall not be afraid of the terror by night,
Nor of the arrow that flies by day."

The footsteps grew louder as the men bounded up the stairwell just outside our flat. Their gruff voices cut through the stillness of the air. Mom gripped Dad's hand, buried her face in his chest, and tried not to make any noise. Had they come for us? Her heart was racing so fast, she felt it would burst out of her chest. Mom tried to focus on the words of hope with promises of protection.

"A thousand may fall at your side,
And ten thousand at your right hand;
But it shall not come near you.
Only with your eyes shall you look,
And see the reward of the wicked."

The sound of pounding boots continued as the men went up another flight of stairs and into the flat directly above ours. Although their words were muffled, their bellowing laughter penetrated the floor and reverberated through our ceiling. *It's as if they're in our flat,* Mom thought to herself. *How are we supposed to feel safe in our home when it's practically inhabited by the military?*

"Because you have made the LORD, who is
      my refuge,
Even the Most High, your dwelling place,
No evil shall befall you,
Nor shall any plague come near your dwelling;
For He shall give His angels charge over you,
To keep you in all your ways."

Suddenly the door to the flat upstairs slammed shut as more footsteps pounded down the stairs. Dad and Mom continued praying.

"Because he has set his love upon Me, therefore I will
    deliver him;…
He shall call upon Me, and I will answer him;
I will be with him in trouble;
I will deliver him and honor him.
With long life I will satisfy him,
And show him My salvation."

The men's raucous voices reverberated through the walls as they bounded down the stairs and out the building. They got into their vehicles and drove off. As suddenly as it had begun, it was over. Dad and Mom let out sighs of relief as they embraced each other in silence. They knew they could not endure living in such an environment much longer.

When morning came, Dad and Mom, still visibly shaken and weary, each prepared to go to work; he to teach in the Zoology Department at Makerere University and she to the nurses' station at Mulago Hospital across the valley. They prayed the words of Psalm 91 before leaving me with the babysitter. I was only seventeen months old at the time and they were increasingly concerned for my safety. Idi Amin's rule over Uganda had ushered in a regime of death. My dad did not want to leave his birth country, his family, or the life he and Mom had built. He had a strong conviction about not giving in to a dictator and failing to stand and fight for what was right. Mom, on the other hand, was frightened by what was going on and was eager to get out while there was still a chance. But when Idi Amin's son moved into the faculty apartment above us, bringing with him his military goons, they knew it was time for the three of us to leave Uganda.

Once the decision was made, they worked on a plan, knowing that while many had tried to flee before and some had made it out, others were caught and imprisoned or never heard from again. My parents did not know how everything would unfold, but they continued to pray for God's guidance.

One day, while walking through campus with the family's safety weighing heavily on his shoulders, Dad ran into a friend who had recently returned from the United States. Peter somberly told Dad that his brother had been murdered and that he was in the process of making arrangements to permanently leave the country and return to the United States, where he planned to attend the University of Minnesota.

The moment Peter said that, it sparked something in Dad, as he had been contemplating the idea of going back to school. He asked Peter to send the application for the University of Minnesota when he returned to the United States. Peter agreed and that was the last time they saw each other in Uganda. Their encounter was the beginning of God's plan for our departure. Once Dad received the university application from Peter, he promptly filled it out and sent it back to him. (This was long before the days of the internet!) Peter turned in the paperwork, which was miraculously reviewed within a matter of two weeks. Dad's acceptance to the university meant we now had a destination. We were going to Duluth, Minnesota.

With the fall term fast approaching, we needed to move quickly. First on the list was obtaining passports, which was not an easy thing to do at the time in Uganda. The average wait was months, sometimes years, and some people never got one. An additional complication was that passport applications were monitored by the government, and it raised red flags when the application was for an entire family. This could potentially place the applicants under surveillance. Despite the obstacles, Dad and Mom were miraculously able to get our passports within a week (without bribing anyone).

The next step in the plan was to get clearance from the appropriate channels to leave the country. Yes, that actually was necessary! Because my parents hoped to one day return to Uganda when it was safe, Dad needed to get approval from the Department of Education to study abroad. It's hard to believe, but authorization from the Undersecretary of Education was also critical for getting any money out of the country. (This was before credit cards were introduced in Uganda!) There was immense risk in seeking this clearance owing to the possibility of the undersecretary or informants on his staff reporting our intentions to the government. However, to Dad's surprise, the undersecretary asked him why he was still in the country, given the impending danger looming over his head. He gave Dad the necessary clearance and bluntly told him to flee the country at the earliest possible opportunity if he wanted to stay alive. He strongly recommended that we not fly out of Entebbe (the main airport) but instead leave Uganda on foot and fly out of the Nairobi airport in Kenya, since that would arouse less suspicion.

Having the undersecretary's authorization gave Dad the ability to purchase our airline tickets. Because of the turmoil in the country, British Airways, the major carrier, no longer came into Uganda, leaving only one airline still flying out of the country. Dad went to their office to buy tickets with the money the undersecretary had approved for him to withdraw and made arrangements to pick up the tickets in Nairobi so we would not need to risk having them confiscated. The plan was finally complete.

Ugandans wanting to flee faced the enormous threat of attempting to get out of the country without being caught. My parents had the additional danger that Idi Amin's son Taban lived above them, and could have them imprisoned or killed. Dad had obtained empty university boxes to pack our belongings. Within a few short days of speaking to the undersecretary, our flat was packed and a secret location to store the boxes was secured. In order to move everything out of the flat without arousing suspicion, Dad got a university truck to make it appear as if things were just being transported for the university. The workers Dad hired arrived about 10:00 a.m., a time selected when most residents were in class and there was little activity around Mitchell Hall. So, in broad daylight, five men worked alongside Dad to swiftly move the boxes from our flat to the truck parked outside the building. When it was fully loaded, they took our belongings to the location Dad had prearranged.

The following morning, a trusted friend picked us up at 5:00 a.m. to take us to the taxi station, and under the cover of darkness, we left Mitchell Hall for the last time. Mom felt a lump in her throat as we drove away. Her heart was breaking from not being able to say goodbye to her mother before fleeing. She lived miles away in another village and was going to be devastated when she found out her only child had left the country. The pain of no longer being able to hold her only grandchild in her arms was going to be too much for her to bear. Mom wiped her tears as she tried to reassure herself that her mother would understand it was for everyone's safety. Because friends and family could be questioned and beaten to reveal what they knew about our disappearance, the less they knew the better.

When we arrived at the taxi station, Dad tended to our bags while Mom scooped me up in her arms and we got into a taxi for the long trip to the town of Busia, located at the Uganda-Kenya border. During the three-and-a-half-hour drive, I bounced around in the back seat, playing with my big white hat, too young to grasp the gravity of the situation. Dad sat in the front of the taxi, completely stoic as he stared into the distance. The weight of protecting his wife and child was heavy on his mind. He could hear me playing in the back seat, and every sound I made reminded him that whether we stayed or fled, my future was at stake. Throughout the long drive, he silently prayed, asking God to protect us as we made our escape. Dad had the taxi driver drop us off a mile outside the border and we got out to walk the rest of the way with the local traders.

Dad found a man with a large wheelbarrow and paid him to carry our luggage. Then he and Mom parted and walked on different sides of the road. This was done intentionally to increase our chances of getting across the border. Dad planned to appear to be traveling alone as a scholar doing research in Kenya. Mom and I would not draw as much attention traveling as just mother and child. The plan was to reconnect as soon as we all crossed the border into Kenya.

When we got to the perimeter of the border, there was a large crowd of people gathered outside the building. Dad retrieved his suitcase and got in line. A little while later Mom got hers from the man with the wheelbarrow. She juggled between holding me and the luggage as we made our way to the line. Soldiers armed with machine guns were an imposing presence keeping an eye on the restless swarm of people. Dad fit the profile the government would be looking for—an educated man wanting to leave the country. As his turn for interrogation came, he debated whether his plan was going to work. He knew he needed to state his case convincingly to be sure the soldiers did not become suspicious. There was so much at stake. So much planning and preparation had led to this very moment.

In preparation to cross the border between Uganda and Kenya, Dad had packed petri dishes from his lab containing tissue samples from infected fish in Lake Victoria. As he was being interrogated, he explained that to examine the fish, he needed to use specialized equipment that was not available in Uganda. Concerned for their food source, the soldiers quickly let him through.

Meanwhile, Mom was having a traumatic experience in the line designated for women.

"Where are you going?" a soldier barked as another one grabbed her suitcase and began rummaging through it.

Mom could not bring herself to look at the man towering over her in his military fatigues. She nervously recited the response she had carefully practiced before they left while trying to keep me from fussing.

"Phew, what is that smell?" one of the men asked as he turned from the suitcase he was searching.

"I think it's coming from that child," another soldier said with disgust as he pointed at me.

"You take the kid while I check the woman," he commanded his peer.

"I don't want that smell on me," the soldier insisted.

Bouncing me up and down in her arms, Mom knew my cloth diaper needed to be changed, but she could not risk getting out of the line at the most crucial part of our journey.

One of the soldiers stepped forward and took me from my mom so she could be searched by the female staff. I shrieked, kicking and desperately flinging my arms toward my mom.

"Grace, it's okay, I'm right here," Mom said, trying to calm me as she was searched.

"Yes, the smell is definitely coming from this child," the soldier announced as he held me at arm's length.

"Well, do something about it. I can't take any more of that smell or the noise!" the other soldier barked.

I let out a high-pitched wail while forcefully lunging my torso toward my mom and trying to get away from the man who was holding me. The soldier thrust me back into my mom's arms and gruffly said, "Just go! Get the child out of here!"

Mom scooped me into her arms, grabbed the suitcase, and continued quickly through the building while trying to calm me.

Mom went through the checkpoint on the Kenya side of the border and quickly found Dad. Eager to leave the border crossing, they found a taxi and we headed straight to Nairobi, where my parents had arranged to stay with a family who had fled Uganda prior to us. We stayed with them while waiting to get visas, which had not been possible in Uganda because the United States Embassy had closed its doors because of all the turmoil happening in the country. Dad sent his tuition to the University of Minnesota and requested a letter from the university stating it had been paid. Once he received the letter, he took it to the United States Embassy in Nairobi. When they saw his documentation of admission and payment, the process was expedited, and they granted us the visas. We departed Nairobi on October 23, 1976. After several connecting flights, we arrived in Minnesota and settled in Duluth.

Several years later, Mom graduated with a BS in food science. Dad completed his PhD and published the findings from the scientific specimen that had helped us cross the border into Kenya. When we fled Uganda in 1976, Idi Amin had been in power only five short years. His regime is remembered for the terror and crimes against humanity inflicted upon his people. By the time he was finally overthrown in 1979 by the invading Tanzanian army, more than three hundred thousand people had been murdered during his administration. We were among those fortunate to have gotten out safely.

It was through that winter storm that we first experienced the Lord as *Jehovah Mephalti*, our deliverer. While we did not build a physical altar upon settling in Duluth, we worshipped the Lord and thanked Him for rescuing us from the regime of Idi Amin. In Psalm 18:2, we see the words David sang after the Lord delivered him from King Saul and his enemies: "The LORD [Jehovah] is my rock, my fortress and my deliverer [Mephalti]; my God is my rock, in whom I take refuge, my shield and the horn of my salvation, my stronghold" (NIV). Just as *Jehovah Mephalti* delivered my parents and me, and just as He delivered David, He is able to deliver you, too. All you need to do is call on Him. You can start by just telling the Lord you need Him. If you are not sure where to go from there, you can simply say the following: "Jesus, I need you. I cannot make it through this winter season on my own. I'm tired of trying and failing. I invite You into my life as my Lord and Savior. Fill me with Your Holy Spirit. Give me the strength and wisdom I need for each new day." If you said that prayer, I would love to hear from you. If you go to my website, I will send you some resources you may find helpful.

Just as some animals migrate during the winter months, we also may need to migrate during a winter chill. For my parents and me, it meant leaving Idi Amin's regime in Uganda. Moses and the Israelites crossed the Red Sea and left the life of slavery in Egypt. Ruth lost her husband and left her people in Moab to go with her mother-in-law, Naomi, to Judah. When God leads us to migrate, we may have to leave our community, job, home, school, or place of comfort. However, we can be encouraged through numerous stories in the Bible that He has so much more for us on the other side.

In addition to migrating, another way that animals adapt to the cold winter season is by adding layers and growing a thick underfur for warmth. Bison not only grow extra fur, but their skin also thickens, and they develop a layer of fat for insulation. As we navigate through life's extended windchills, it is important for us to develop a thick skin and keep a tender heart. That takes work. It's much easier to have thin skin and a hardened heart when haters talk trash about you or stab you in the back. When you find out through social media that a friend did not invite you to the party. When someone else is the star at the office and your work is not recognized or appreciated. When you move to a new school, a new job, or a new community and no one tries to get to know you because they are too busy and already have their social network. When friends and family leave you hanging or judge how you are living your life. When you long to be part of a friendship, relationship, family, or community but they are not open to embracing you. When you are on the outside looking in and watching everyone live their best lives. It is in such seasons that we have got to intentionally work at developing a thick skin and keeping a tender heart.

A while back, someone said something to me that was vile, attacking my character, discrediting all of who I am, what I have overcome, and what I've accomplished in life. Their poisonous words completely blindsided me and left me struggling to breathe for days. As I continuously replayed the poisonous words in my head, I could feel my heart begin to harden.

I knew I needed to stop the process that was causing me to wither instead of flourish. There are a few things I've done over the years to develop a thick skin and keep a tender heart. I remind myself that people throughout history who have done great things have always been talked about. It's important not to let other people's negative words and actions throw you off course. We need to do what Jesus did when He went back to His hometown and the mob tried to kill Him: He walked right through the crowd and went on His way. In other words, let them talk as you go about your business walking in your purpose. The person who follows the crowd will go no farther than the crowd. The one who walks alone is likely to find themselves in places no one has ever been before.

People often throw shade because of their own insecurities. In order to feel better about themselves, they tear someone else down. Don't allow yourself to stoop down to their level. You are an eagle, created to soar; not to engage with turkeys on the ground. Did you know that while many animals are slowing down and going into hibernation, bald eagles are mating and laying their eggs? They do this so that by the time summer arrives, they will be teaching their young how to hunt when prey is abundant and easier to catch. Definitely not what the turkeys are doing! Just as we see in nature, we weather the winter windchills of life by adding layers—specifically by developing a thicker skin while maintaining a tender heart.

Animals that do not migrate or prepare for the cold through such measures as developing thicker layers of fur have another way to adapt for winter. They hide in a den or burrow and go into a deep sleep known as hibernation. Their heart rate and body temperature lower to save energy until they wake up in the spring. While burrowing down for an extended nap can sound appealing during difficult seasons in our life, that is not the takeaway for us here. Rather, we will look at the wisdom of slowing down and being still.

A while back, Phil and I had a guest come and stay with us for a few days. Normally, with just the two of us in the house, our home is very peaceful. The house sits on a few acres surrounded by majestic trees and overlooking a small lake. We frequently see different species of birds from hawks to Canada geese to blue herons. There are plenty of fish, turtles, deer, and an occasional fox sighting. We selected the home with the intention to open it up as a peaceful haven for friends and family to enjoy the beauty of God's creation. A place where they can get away from the busyness of the world, rest, and spend time in the Lord's presence. What struck me about this particular guest was the unusual amount of noise their phone was making from constant notifications. There were chimes and buzzes for emails, texts, social media posts from all platforms, and a host of other alerts. Although our guest was on vacation, the world kept screaming for their attention. I found myself getting stressed by the nonstop noise. There was barely a moment when their phone was silenced to allow them to be fully present. I really wished I could press "Mute" on the gadget so they could experience the breathtaking natural world around them instead of scrolling through everyone else's highlight reel. Studies have shown that seeing birds, shrubs, and trees can help improve mental health.

In moments when I am overwhelmed or stuck in a winter chill of life, I have found it tremendously helpful to go sit outside and be still. I focus on using each of my senses one by one to take in the natural world around me. I often start by closing my eyes and taking some deep breaths to take in the fresh air. Then with my eyes still closed, I listen to the sounds around me. The wind blowing through the trees, the birds that are chirping, and the many squirrels scurrying about. Then I open my eyes and look at the trees around me, the sky above me, and the ground below me. Depending on the weather, you might enjoy taking off your shoes and feeling the grass under your feet. Sometimes, I will whisper a prayer and thank God for His creation. Most of the time, I sit or stand very still and just take in the natural world around me. I look at the birds and think about how they are not worried or stressed. God has not stopped providing for their needs. Matthew 6:25–27 tells us, "Therefore I tell you, do not worry about your life, what you will eat or drink; or about your body, what you will wear. Is not life more than food, and the body more than clothes? Look at the birds of the air; they do not sow or reap or store away in barns, and yet your heavenly Father feeds them. Are you not much more valuable than they? Can any one of you by worrying add a single hour to your life?" (NIV).

Every time I look at trees, I meditate on how secure and calm they are. It's how I want to be in a winter chill. They make me think of

Isaiah 61:3: "They will be called oaks of righteousness, a planting of the LORD for the display of his splendor" (NIV). That is what I want to be. A child of God who displays His splendor. My desire is that the words that I speak and how I carry myself are a reflection of Him. My prayer is that they draw people to Him and give Him all the glory.

Trees that have fallen due to age, disease, or a storm add enchanting character to the forest. Sometimes we, too, go through a season in life where we have fallen. Whether because of our actions, the decisions of others, or a divine intervention, the book of Job lets us know that God is with us, and able to restore us. Job 14:7–9 assures us, "For there is hope for a tree, When it is cut down, that it will sprout again, And its shoots will not fail. Though its roots grow old in the ground, And its stump dies in the dry soil, At the scent of water it will flourish And produce sprigs like a plant" (NASB). If the winter windchill knocks us down, we can be encouraged that it is not the final story. There is still hope for a better future. There is hope after that decision you made. There is hope after your divorce. There is freedom from your addiction. There is healing in your estranged family relationship. Life will sprout again. With some water and *Son*shine, it always does. My friend, you will flourish again.

But what do you do until that time? What do you *do* while weathering the winter windchills? What do you *do* in a prolonged and challenging, never-ending season? When your dreams seem dead, you feel alone or overlooked, and your life is not as you envisioned it would be. What do you *do* while hibernating, developing a thick skin, and keeping a tender heart? When you don't want to get out of bed in the morning because the situation still has not changed? When you go about your day like a lifeless shell carrying an illness that will not go away? What do you *do* when you are stuck at the crossroads of unknown and unexpected paths? In such times I have found it helpful to *do* two things: Draw near to Jesus and abide in Him. With whatever little energy and strength I have, I focus it all on drawing near to Jesus and abiding in Him. Just like the woman with the issue of blood, I know that if I can just touch the hem of His garment, if I can just get myself in the presence of the Lord, He has everything I need. He meets me in my loneliness and depression and lets me know He is with me. He assures me He is for me and will never leave me. He is my source of strength and is fighting for me. He is constant in a world that is ever changing. He is love in a society full of rising tension, hate, prejudice, crime, cancel culture, and fear. He has the answers to my questions and wisdom for my situation. He takes my stress and anxiety and gives me His peace. He provides comfort and healing for my broken heart. He takes my heartache, longing, and despair and gives me hope and joy. He takes my confusion and gives me clarity and purpose.

Colossians 1:16 explains, "For everything, absolutely everything, above and below, visible and invisible...everything got started in him and finds its purpose in him" (MSG).

In Him is where and how we find our purpose. Everything comes from Him, was created by Him, exists through Him and for Him. The meaning, direction, answers, and purpose we are looking for is all in Him. And He wants to reveal it to us. All we need to do is simply draw near and abide in Him.

James, the half-brother of Jesus, tells us, "Draw near to God and He will draw near to you" (James 4:8 NKJV).

Isn't it encouraging to know that the God who created the universe promises to come close to you as you come close to Him? Not only that, but according to John 15:4, as you abide in Him, you will bear fruit.

"Abide in me, and I in you. As the branch cannot bear fruit by itself, unless it abides in the vine, neither can you, unless you abide in me" (ESV). Abiding in Christ means living in union with Him. It's experiencing His daily and hourly presence. It's intimacy, connection, and fellowship with the Lord.

All throughout the Bible, people experienced transformation, meaning, purpose, and miracles as they drew near to Jesus and abided in Him. One of the many characters who continues to impact me is Paul. Originally known as Saul, he was zealously persecuting followers of Christ. Then he had an encounter with Jesus on a Damascus road (Acts 9:1–22). Soon after, he became an evangelist and was the target of persecution. He continued to draw near to God as people tried to kill him, and continued to abide in the Lord while in jail as he encouraged people to rejoice in the Lord. He truly is a remarkable example for us to learn from!

But how do you draw near and abide if you were never taught? I'm so glad you asked!

I think it might help to think about what you do when you want to get to know someone special. You talk with each other and share about your backgrounds, interests, what brings you joy, and what frustrates you or breaks your heart. You spend time together and introduce them to your friends. You prioritize them, answer whenever they call, and help however they need it. As the relationship grows and becomes more significant, you introduce each other to your families. You increasingly open your heart to each other and begin talking about sharing a future together.

In a similar way, we draw near to God by talking with Him and spending time with Him. We get to know Him by reading the Bible through which we see His love for us and His desire to be with us. We learn what pleases Him and what causes Him heartache and pain. We begin to prioritize Him, not out of obligation as we check off a daily reading list, but out of a desire to be with Him. Daily finding out what is on His heart and mind. You answer when He whispers that He wants to be with you. It might be a brief moment in your day when you stop and say, "Thank You, God," or "I love You, Lord," or "I'm so grateful for You," or "You mean everything to me," just as you would pause and send a text to someone you love. Some people call these ten-second prayers "breath prayers" or "flash prayers." Whether you are expressing your love to God or praying a short prayer for someone, either way you are abiding with the Lord. And that is where I want to be. I would rather be unknown in this world and known to God than known in this world and unknown to God. He is the One that we will be spending eternity with!

Drawing near to God and abiding in Him is not limited to our "quiet time" or moments of personal devotion. Yes, spending time alone with God is important to our spiritual growth and relationship with Him. But there is so much more we can experience as we continually draw near and consistently abide in Him. The Lord longs to be part of everything we do. We can invite Him to do just that. I was first introduced to this concept years ago through a seventeenth-century book written by Brother Lawrence. In *Practicing the Presence of God,* he wrote about how as a cook in a French monastery, he turned his routine and menial tasks into acts of praise and communion with God. He began preparing meals and washing dishes *with* God and *for* God. He recognized that God is always intimately present with us, and he cultivated an awareness of His presence by continually talking with Him.

This started as Brother Lawrence read numerous resources on how to go to God and how to practice the spiritual life. None of them were helpful in showing him how to become wholly God's. So, he resolved "to give all for ALL. Then I gave myself wholly to God; I renounced everything that was not His. I did this to deal with my sins, and because of my love for Him. *I began to live as if there were nothing,* *absolutely nothing but Him.* So upon this earth I began to seek to live as though there were only the Lord and me in the whole world."*

In his book *The Purpose Driven Life*, Rick Warren puts it this way: "What you normally do for yourself you begin doing for God, whether it is eating, bathing, working, relaxing, or taking out the trash. Today we often feel we must 'get away' from our daily routine in order to worship God, but that is only because we haven't learned to practice his presence all the time. Brother Lawrence found it easy to worship God through the common tasks of life; he didn't have to go away for spiritual retreats. This is God's ideal."**

One key way we can do this is by uttering short conversational prayers throughout the day as we previously discussed. Another is by thinking about God's Word and meditating on it throughout your day. We often have different understandings of meditation based on our backgrounds. To help bring some clarity, you can think of meditation as focused thinking. Eastern meditation focuses on emptying the mind whereas Christian meditation focuses on filling our minds—specifically with the Word of God. When we think about God's Word over and over, that's meditation. It might sound difficult to do, but when we worry, we are actually meditating on our problems over and over. You will begin to flourish as you meditate and think about what God's Word says about your problem rather than consuming all your energy in worrying about the problem.

Rick Warren explains:

Practicing the presence of God is a skill, a habit you can develop. Just as musicians practice scales every day in order

---

* Brother Lawrence and Frank Laubach, *Practicing His Presence*, ed. Gene Edwards (Jacksonville, Fl.: SeedSowers Publishing, 1973), p. 59.
** Rick Warren, *The Purpose Driven Life* (Grand Rapids, Mi.: Zondervan, 2002), p. 88.

to play beautiful music with ease, you must force yourself to think about God at different times in your day. You must train your mind to remember God.

At first you will need to create reminders to regularly bring your thoughts back to the awareness that God is with you in that moment. Begin by placing visual reminders around you. You might post little notes that say, "God is with me and for me right now!" Benedictine monks use the hourly chimes of a clock to remind them to pause and pray "the hour prayer." If you have a watch or cell phone with an alarm, you could do the same. Sometimes you will sense God's presence; other times you won't. If you are seeking an *experience* of his presence through all of this, you have missed the point. We don't praise God to feel good, but to *do* good. Your goal is not a feeling, but a continual awareness of the *reality* that God is always present.*

Another author who wrote on the subject in the twentieth century is Frank C. Laubach. He said:

We shall not become like Christ until we give Him more time. A teachers' college requires students to attend classes for twenty-five hours a week for three years. Could it prepare competent teachers or a law school prepare competent lawyers if they studied only ten minutes a week? Neither can Christ, and he never pretended that he could. To his disciples he said: "Come with me, walk with me, talk and listen to me, work and rest with me, eat and sleep with me, twenty-four hours a

---

* Rick Warren, *The Purpose Driven Life* (Grand Rapids, Mi.: Zondervan, 2002), pp. 89–90.

day for three years." That was their college course—"He chose them," the Bible says, "that they might be with him," 168 hours a week!*

While I am nowhere near that, I make it my goal to draw near to God and abide in Him.

I believe it is in our **DNA** to **D**raw **N**ear & **A**bide.

Draw
Near &
Abide

How do I know that? Before I explain, let me ask you to think about when you recently met someone for the first time. Was it in the middle of a crowded lobby, on a Zoom meeting, or a phone call? Wherever it was, I imagine there was some type of communication as you saw each other face to face or heard each other's voices. Otherwise, that would make for a very unusual introduction. But that is exactly what happened when two particular people in the Bible met each other for the first time. Luke chapter one tells the story of two women in the same extended family who become pregnant for the first time. After the angel Gabriel told Mary that she "will be with child and give birth to a son" whom she is to name Jesus (Luke 1:31 NIV), Gabriel tells her that her relative Elizabeth is also going to have a child. Mary travels from Nazareth in Galilee to a town in the hill country of Judea to see her relative.

When Elizabeth heard Mary's greeting, the baby leaped in her womb, and Elizabeth was filled with the Holy Spirit. In a loud

---

* Frank Laubach, *The Game with Minutes* (Mansfield Centre, Ct.: Martino Publishing, 2012), pp. 3–4.

voice she exclaimed: "Blessed are you among women, and blessed is the child you will bear! But why am I so favored, that the mother of my Lord should come to me? As soon as the sound of your greeting reached my ears, the baby in my womb leaped for joy. Blessed is she who has believed that the Lord would fulfill his promises to her!" (Luke 1:41–45 NIV)

John the Baptist and Jesus' first meeting was spiritual. They did not see each other, shake hands, or hug each other. They were in two separate wombs in two separate bodies, not even able to speak yet. But something happened when they were in each other's presence. John recognized the presence of the Holy. The Bible said he leapt for joy in his mother's womb. I'm pretty sure that would not have happened if John was "meeting" any other cousins or nephews who were still in their mother's womb. John's reaction was physical and spiritual. This tells me that while we are in the womb, before we can see or speak, our spirit recognizes God's Spirit. There is a connection because not only did He create us, He created us in His likeness. Long before we are born, we are wired to draw near to God. It's in our DNA to **D**raw **N**ear and **A**bide with the Lord. That is how we weather the prolonged winter windchills. That is how we find purpose in the unknown and unexpected seasons of life. That is how we flourish. So, the next time a friend asks if you have taken one of those DNA tests to discover your genetic heritage, you can answer them and then ask if they know their spiritual heritage and DNA.

These days, when I meet someone for the first time, I ask the Lord to help me know them spiritually, not just with what I see or hear them say. I ask Him to help me see what He sees in the spiritual so that I don't just rely on what little I experience in the natural. This has been so valuable when deciding who to work with or who to open up to. I highly recommend it for anyone who is dating or engaged! God knows that person way better than you do! Just something from your friend Grace to consider. I'm looking out for you!

As we wrap up this section on the winter seasons of life, know that I have been praying for you as you were reading these chapters. You are going to make it through this storm. God's got you! If you are not currently in a winter season, it *is* unfortunately in the forecast of life. I encourage you to take the time to assemble an emergency pack as we discussed. Be prepared for life's unexpected storms by getting the Word of God in you—don't wait and scramble to learn a Scripture in the middle of an emotional blizzard. Create a worship playlist—perhaps one that is geared toward fighting spiritual battles and another that leans toward being at peace in His presence. Be intentional in developing a couple of safe, deep friendships, and look into finding a licensed therapist. For those in the middle of a windchill, work on developing a thick skin while keeping a tender heart. When stressed, anxious, or feeling some kind of way, practice being still and taking inspiration from nature. And in the waiting, do not "slam on the brakes" and put your life on hold. Create a vision for what you are believing for in the summer and find hope in that. Live into your vision by taking steps to flourish mentally, emotionally, financially, physically, and spiritually. Focusing on serving, encouraging, and blessing others will bring a sense of joy and fulfillment in the midst of the winter. And rest assured that the season will eventually change. Until then, make every effort to embrace your spiritual DNA by Drawing Near and Abiding in Him. I am believing for great things for you as we move on to the spring and the summer seasons.

PART 3

SPRING

unearthed from my journals:

8/7/06—excerpt from a letter from Neil Clark Warren, founder of eHarmony.com

Dear Grace:

It was an absolutely heaven-sent experience to meet with you this morning while walking around the Rose Bowl. Was there any doubt in your mind that God had that experience in mind for the two of us today? I am sending you with this letter two of my books. There are others should you choose to read them. It would be my delight to have you ask for them....

Now don't forget. You are going to work your way through *Date...or Soul Mate?*, get everything clear about yourself, and give me a call. We will walk the Rose Bowl again and solve these easy things. Then, we will together hunt for that person with whom you can safely entrust your heart for a lifetime.

We are all in this together with God.

With great love,

Neil

1/10/15

I believe the Lord is speaking to me that I need to make room for my husband in my home. Just like the woman made room for her blessing of oil by getting as many empty jars as she could, I need to do likewise.

3/17/16—word from a friend

It is going to happen very soon and the Lord is going to surprise you. People will look with raised eyebrows as to how fast it is happening.

2/22/17

Joel Osteen was talking about Philip and the Ethiopian. Philip came out of nowhere to answer the Ethiopian's question. Joel was saying that Philips are coming into our lives. Thank you, Lord, I receive it!

CHAPTER 7

Planted Through the Process

As trees come out of the winter season, their roots grow quickly to find new nutrients and water. The process takes time and work, and is something we can learn from. So often we are tempted to skip the difficult processes of growing and establishing in our rush to get to greener pastures. A tree cannot bypass the process of finding water; it cannot simply transplant itself somewhere that looks lush with water and nutrients. That is not what they do. Trees remain planted and continue to establish their roots. However, because we cannot see what is taking place underground, we get impatient that things are not progressing as fast as we would like. We are tempted to take things into our own hands and transplant ourselves somewhere else. That is where I found myself when I turned forty.

I was done. Specifically, I was done with being single. I was done with guys who were afraid of commitment and the ones who were intimidated by a woman in leadership. I was done with going on dates, only to look into eyes that glazed over the minute I answered their questions about what I did for a living. I was done with waiting for God. The loneliness, heartache, and frustration I felt at this stage was unbearable. It seemed like I had been in a winter season forever and I was losing hope in God to answer my prayers. I was ready to take matters into my own hands.

The way I saw it, one of the main obstacles to me getting a second date was the fact that I was a minister. My profession worked to my benefit if I needed an exit strategy during an awkward blind date. However, it was discouraging to see how it became a deal breaker for some guys before they even got to know me. It was so frustrating that they could not see past the pastor title. And that just because I was a minister, it did not mean that I was some sort of unemotional, untouchable being. I was a woman first. But somehow so many men did not see that, and I knew something needed to change. I wrestled with the fact that I felt called to ministry, but at the same time I did not want to spend the rest of my life single. After agonizing over it incessantly, I came up with the perfect plan where I could still do ministry, but do it from behind the scenes instead of on a public platform. I had started taking real estate investment classes and found that people's eyes lit up when I said I was an investor. Since I love to be generous and bless people, I came up with a win-win solution. I would use the money I made from real estate investing to fund ministries and churches. My ultimate goal was to become a philanthropist. I wanted to make enough money to be able to hand pastors a substantial check for a church building. This would mean they did not have to worry about raising funds, but could instead just focus on pastoring people. In my plan, I would still be doing ministry; it would just be behind the scenes as I funded the visions and dreams of others. I did not need to be the one on the platform. I reasoned that I would still be fulfilling my purpose as I empowered others in their ministries. I felt my plan was solid. I was excited to go on dates and see people lean in with interest when I said I was an investor.

About that time, international speaker and author Bob Goff was having his first Dream Big Workshop. It was designed to help people overcome obstacles and accomplish their dreams. I thought it would be the perfect place to shift gears and start my journey toward becoming a real estate investor and eventually a philanthropist. However, on the second day of the seminar, Bob called me out in the room of forty people. He said, "Grace, you have something to say, and people need to hear your voice." I thought for sure he had confused me with someone else in the room. People were there wanting to build their platform to speak, write, and launch nonprofits…I was running from mine. The reality was I was trying to run away from my seemingly never-ending winter season of singleness and plant myself somewhere where I thought I would flourish. Not only did Bob call me out, but he invited me to speak with him at an event he was keynoting that week. The following week, when he found out I was writing a book, he told me he would write the foreword for my future book. So much for my "behind the scenes" plan!

Just before the Dream Big Workshop, I had been at a major cross-road and ready to walk away from my purpose. I was sure it was preventing me from finding love. I was trying to cut the winter season short and skip to summer instead of letting things follow their natural course. Thankfully, the seminar brought perspective and a renewed commitment to embrace the season I was in. I made a conscious decision to be open to new things, even if they did not go with my plan. Four months later, I met my husband, Phil, when he came to work with our church. (More on that later in the book.) I would not have met him if I had run from my winter season, skipped the spring, and tried to enter summer by changing careers. Because I stayed planted in ministry and opened my mind to all that came in the spring season, I was right where I needed to be when God had our paths cross.

Without roots, trees would not be able to survive. Not only do they make up the base of the tree, but they absorb water, minerals, and nutrients for its survival. Roots also store the nutrients for the tree to use during the cold winter months. Probably what roots are most known for is for anchoring trees to the ground. This is what prevents them from falling during storms or flying away because of heavy winds. Like trees, we need to grow and maintain strong roots that keep us anchored during the seasons of life. We do this through absorbing the Word of God and being in His presence. "So then, just as you received Christ Jesus as Lord, continue to live your lives in him, *rooted and built up in him*, strengthened in the faith as you were taught and overflowing with thankfulness" (Colossians 2:6–7 NIV, emphasis added). We develop our roots through worship, prayer, fasting, Bible study, and staying in community with other believers. The deeper and broader our spiritual roots go, the more we are able to withstand the trials, troubles, and storms of life.

As we continue living our lives in Christ, being rooted and built up in Him, we will begin to grow deeper roots. Roots that will establish yourself in the soil structure in such a way that you develop a new depth of security and peace. Things that cause others to waver and fall will not be able to move you because your root system is strong. You will not be uprooted when unexpected storms erupt in your world. You will not be thrown off by the winds of the unknown. The relentless struggles of life will not be able to knock you down. You will not attempt to transplant, at the first sign of drama, to another plot of soil where the grass looks greener. Your deep roots will absorb nutrients that will enable you to stand secure with an assuredness of God's faithfulness in the midst of the unknown and unexpected seasons of life. You will stand secure while waiting for your answer to prayer. You will stand secure while believing for that big opportunity, believing to get married, believing to get pregnant, believing for healing, believing for that loved one to come to Christ. You, my friend, will not waver but will continue to stand secure while waiting for God's direction, while listening for His voice, and while seeking His will.

Tree roots continue to grow no matter what things look like aboveground. In other words, their growth and security are not dependent on what the tree is seeing in its environment. In the same way, I believe you are going to continue to grow deep roots and stand secure regardless of what your eyes are seeing taking place around you. I have to admit such roots do not develop overnight, like in a time lapse video. But we can trust that something is happening even if we cannot see it with our natural eye.

Take, for example, the acacia tree, a well-known landmark in the African savanna. It can grow up to 18 meters tall and live up to 200 years. What's even more impressive is what is taking place in the underground part of a tree. Trees start with a taproot that grows straight down below the trunk of the tree, providing stability and absorption. The taproot for acacias can grow nearly 200 feet below the surface, allowing it to access deep groundwater sources and live in extremely dry climates. For context, many trees never establish a taproot, but instead grow a lateral network of roots to depths of only 12 to 24 inches. Trees will show very little visible growth aboveground in their first years of life as their taproots are growing down. As we go through winter seasons in life and navigate unknown paths and unexpected obstacles, it can seem like nothing is happening. Like we are not making any progress. But I want to encourage you that there is something happening underground that you can't see. There's something happening inside you as you are staying planted. Your resilience is growing stronger as you establish deep roots. Roots that keep you planted and prevent you from faltering at the first sign of a storm, the unexpected betrayal of a friend, or a future that is unknown. The world around you may be unstable and unclear, but your taproot system is solid.

Jeremiah 17:7–8 promises, "But blessed is the one who trusts in the LORD, whose confidence is in him. They will be like a tree planted by the water that sends out its roots by the stream. It does not fear when heat comes; its leaves are always green. It has no worries in a year of drought and never fails to bear fruit" (NIV). Psalm 92:12–14 assures us, "The righteous will flourish like a palm tree, they will grow like a cedar of Lebanon; planted in the house of the LORD, they will flourish in the courts of our God. They will still bear fruit in old age, they will stay fresh and green" (NIV). The Cambridge Dictionary states that to "plant" is to "put something firmly and strongly in a particular place." Something that is planted is not wavering or feeble. Unlike leaves in the fall, it is not carried off by the wind. Rather, it is secure when the wind is blowing. It is secure when the rain is pouring. It is secure because long before there was something for the wind to sway or the rain to drench, there was a bedrock that was built underground. A root system that experienced God's provision of water and nutrients for growth. An established web of roots able to say, come what may, we are staying planted in God's presence. A foundation that enables the tree to weather the seasons and continue to thrive. Like trees, we flourish as we plant and establish ourselves in God's presence, placing our trust and confidence in Him.

Spring brings warmer temperatures and longer daylight hours. Buds begin to open and new leaves grow. Birds are chirping, flowers are blooming, and new life is being formed. In the spring season, we want to be open to what God is doing, because it may not look like what we had envisioned. We want to open our minds to new experiences and to doing new things. Perhaps it's going back to school and getting a degree, writing a book, launching a business, or starting a nonprofit. God delights in doing new things, and it gives Him great pleasure to have us be part of them. It is His character. Isaiah 43:19 says, "Behold, I am doing a new thing!" (ESV). However, His plans often do not make sense to our finite minds. They defy logic and require us to be open to a different way of thinking. But as we engage, more often than not, we get to experience something pretty remarkable.

The Bible is filled with stories of people who needed to be open to new things in order to experience all that God had for them. Noah was open to building an ark when there was no sign of rain, and because of that, he saved his entire family. Abraham was open to leaving everything and going to a land he did not know. The Lord blessed him and made him the father of nations. Rahab was open to hiding the spies, and as a result, her family was spared. Gideon was open to decreasing his army from 32,000 to 300 when fighting the Midianite army, and because of that, God not only led them to victory, but there was peace in the land for forty years. Ruth was open to following her mother-in-law, and because of that, she met her husband. Mary was open to the message from the angel Gabriel and became the mother of Jesus. The list of people is endless.

From their stories, it's clear that being open enables us to discover our purpose and participate in God's story. It is a life of adventure. No amount of planning or orchestration comes close to what happens when we join Him. His journey leads us out of our comfort zones and broadens our horizons. We learn about ourselves—the insecurities, fears, wounds, pride, jealousy, and other things we did not realize were there. We start to heal and grow as we journey with him and experience His character. Our minds and thoughts transform, and our faith begins to overshadow our fears. Our anxieties fade, and our moods are uplifted as we see the world around us through different lenses. We gain new perspectives and a new sense of purpose for our lives. Not only do we often meet new and interesting people along the way, but we experience a deeper level of fulfillment. And many of us make memories that last a lifetime.

After Phil and I got married, I moved across the country to live with him in Charlotte, North Carolina. Coming from California, where there had been years of drought and mountain fires, I was struck by how lush the landscape was. I didn't realize trees could be so green. In the absence of the LA smog, I thought I was going to enjoy breathing the fresh, clean air. However, shortly after I moved, my eyes began to water, burn, and itch incessantly. At first I thought I was having a delayed allergic reaction to the lash extensions I had put on for the wedding. I quickly ruled that out as I began sneezing and constantly having to blow my nose. And if things couldn't get any worse, as a newlywed just back from her honeymoon, I also had an eczema breakout. For those of you who are so fortunate not to know what eczema is, it is a chronic inflammatory skin condition that causes extreme itching, irritation, and inflammation. But as my fellow eczema sufferers can tell you, it is basically when your skin is screaming at you for some unknown reason. It could be because of something you ate, a lotion, a scent, a fabric material, a chemical, metals, dyes, soap, detergents, dust, or even emotions such as stress. The list is endless. And the frustration is high. With each breakout, you begin a seemingly endless elimination process to get to the root cause. It takes time and a whole lot of patience. And as days go by without an answer, it raises stress levels, which triggers yet another breakout in the crazy eczema cycle. I avoided going outside to do anything because my skin was itching so badly. The thought of triggering another episode of itchy, watery eyes and sneezing was just not worth it. If I absolutely needed to go somewhere, I made sure I was fully covered with long sleeves, gloves, a hat, and long pants.

At some point in my misery, someone pointed to a yellow film that was covering everything outside and suggested that it may be the cause of my anguish. In the midst of sneezing, itching, and dealing with burning eyes, I had not really noticed the yellow powder covering cars, sidewalks, and buildings. It was everywhere I looked in my new environment. The minute I made the connection, I knew the yellow dust had to be the cause. It had not crossed my mind to ask about potential allergens before moving. After all, who discusses pollen during premarital counseling sessions? And yet, pollen became the key focus of our first few weeks of marriage as we looked for allergists, dermatologists, and most of all, a resolution. Now that I'm a few years in, I have a medicine cabinet that rivals CVS and my dermatologist's office. I'm determined not to stay closed up in my home and miss out on the beauty of spring because of all that's in the air.

Just as the pollen at first prevented me from going outside and enjoying my life, there are often things that prevent us from enjoying the spring season of life and opening up to new experiences. Probably the strongest one is our feeling of fear. While fear can be used to protect us, in many cases it cripples us. It prevents us from trying new things and reaching our full potential. We're afraid of failure. We hold ourselves back from new things because we're convinced we will fail at them. We're afraid of the unknown. We are concerned about the investment, the consequences, and the worst-case scenarios. We're also afraid of embarrassing ourselves, being misunderstood, or getting canceled. We hold ourselves back from new and unfamiliar situations where we might experience public shame or humiliation.

In addition to feelings of fear, another obstacle is our thoughts: *I don't fit the mold, I won't be good at it*. We tell ourselves, *You don't look like a business owner, an athlete, a leader*, or whatever it is we are trying to step into. We fear everyone will look at us and say, "Who does she think she is?" and "What is she thinking?" We put unrealistic pressure on ourselves to excel at something we've never tried before. We don't give ourselves grace in the learning curve of new experiences.

Sometimes the hurdle is our past experiences. I used to get so upset when people would say, "If you don't get out more, the only person you will meet is the FedEx guy." Often the person "trying to help" me had married their childhood sweetheart and had no idea how challenging it was to "just get out there." They did not know what it was like to connect with someone on a dating app, only to find when you met them in person that they looked nothing like the picture they had posted. They did not know the frustration of getting your hair done, nails done, waxing, selecting an amazing outfit, putting on full makeup, and getting your hopes up, only to be on yet another disappointing blind date. They did not know the heartache of thinking you had really connected with someone after several dates, only to find out they were seeing someone else. Yes, it is hard to be open to new things when previous experiences have not gone well.

We know there are great things that come in the spring season; but how do we remove the barriers so we can enjoy them? It's not like we can go to a pharmacy to pick up allergy medicine for toxic thoughts, emotions, and past experiences. I have found that a great place to learn how to address such challenges is the Bible. It is full of stories that we can glean wisdom from and get a "prescription" to help us embrace the spring seasons of life. There are people who overcame their fears, changed the limiting thoughts they had about themselves, and did not let their past block their future. Their openness allowed them to experience something special that has been recorded in Biblical history. That's what happened for a handful of people who, unbeknownst to them, were working at a wedding Jesus attended.

The apostle John tells about the time Jesus attended a wedding with His disciples before He started His public ministry. At some point during the celebration, the wine ran out. Jesus' mom was also at the wedding, and when she found out the wine was gone, she brought it to His attention. He asked her why she involved Him in the matter, saying His time had not yet come. She didn't respond to Him, but instead told the servers to follow whatever instructions He gave them. Jesus told them to fill some jars with water, and after they'd finished, He had them draw some out and take it to the master of the banquet. Having read the story before, we know the water had been turned into wine, but the servants didn't know that at the moment. For all they knew, they were about to experience the biggest humiliation and cancellation from all future work. To get a better appreciation and understanding of what happened, let's put it in the context of today's workplace.

I imagine it would be like having a job as an entry-level employee and being asked to pull a report off the printer for the CEO of the company and take it to them at a presentation they are hosting for other executives. If all that came out of the printer were blank pieces of paper, could you really put them in a folder and take them to the CEO in the boardroom or auditorium? What if you kept opening the folder as you walked down the hallway and all you saw were empty sheets of paper? Could you really hand it to the CEO? That's the position the servants were in. Jesus has asked them to do something that did not make sense in the natural. There was a lot on the line. It's not like they had seen Him work numerous miracles before!

The beautiful thing about this story is that because of their obedience and faith, it was the servants who got to be a part of the first miracle Jesus performed. The servants had no idea that was going to happen; they were just open to doing something that did not make sense because it was what Jesus had asked them to do. I wonder what miracles the Lord is inviting us to experience with Him as we open to what He wants to do in and through our lives.

There are several things we can learn from this passage about opening up to new experiences.

Say "yes"

Say "yes" to something you have been talking yourself out of. Say "yes" to being open, to being curious, to taking a risk, to learning more about yourself and the world around you, to growing, and to doing something new. Say "yes" to what the Lord is prompting you to do. It's remarkable to see how open the servants were to take direction from a complete stranger. They did not know who Jesus was or what He was able to do, and they said yes. Some of us who know Jesus—myself included—who have been walking with Him for a while still question or challenge Him when He prompts us to do something. Saying "yes" opens us up to new opportunities and experiences. It allows us to receive what the spring season brings so we can someday thoroughly revel in the summer season. What is one new thing that you can say "yes" to today? I encourage you to say it out loud and write it down in a journal with the date next to it. If that comes easily for you, take the next step to a week of saying "yes." Then try it for a month, followed by a year of saying "yes." It is the greatest adventure to begin to live a life of saying "yes" to the Lord. That is how you begin to experience a new depth of purpose. As you die to self daily and engage in *His* will, you will flourish.

Invite others to join you on the journey

When we're scared of opening up to something new, we often come up with "what if" or worst-case scenarios. If you're nervous about trying something new because you keep imagining everything that can go wrong, invite a friend to join you in the process. The servants at the wedding filled the water jars together. They most likely freaked out together over what Jesus asked them to do. And as they obeyed despite their apprehension, they got to experience a once-in-a-lifetime miracle together. There is a beautiful sense of camaraderie that comes from experiencing new things with others.

Years ago, when I set out to buy my first home by myself, I was so overwhelmed. I did not understand the process, the terminology, or where to start. I agonized over the many things that could go wrong—buying at the wrong time or in a community that was not safe, falling in love with a house that did not have good resale value, discovering hidden issues in the property or neighborhood, and getting in over my head financially. The list went on and on and almost prevented me from opening up to buying a home.

Thankfully, I had a number of friends in the business, and it made all the difference to have them come alongside me as my realtor, notary, and mortgage broker. They supported and encouraged me throughout the whole process from looking at houses, signing loan docs, and moving in. We sometimes avoid asking people to help us because we don't want to inconvenience them. However, I have found that true friends enjoy being part of the process. It creates special memories and opportunities to together see God move in ways none of you will forget. To this day, my friends and I talk about the miracle we all experienced when God blessed me with a home. They were so grateful to have been a part of that because it stirred their faith to believe Him for greater things. What about you? Who are two or three people you can invite to be part of your journey in saying "yes" to God and believing Him for greater things? I encourage you to reach out to them. They will thank you for the opportunity to be part of seeing and experiencing God move.

Take one step at a time

Notice that Jesus told the servants to "draw some [water] out and *take it* to the master of the banquet" (John 2:8 NIV, emphasis added). This was not an open bar where people would come up and order their drink. The servants had to physically take the drink to the master of the banquet. I imagine that may have been daunting. But they did it by taking one step at a time. It can be intimidating to try something new. You're not sure if you will do it correctly or if you will be able to complete it. If you can relate, I encourage you to think of overcoming your fear and crippling thoughts as a staircase—take it one step at a time.

For example, if you want to complete a marathon, it's daunting to think of running 26.2 miles. Instead, it's helpful to start with a walk around the neighborhood or track. Put together a fun playlist or ask a friend to join you. Before you know it, you will have walked four times around the track and completed your first mile! As you continue to do that, you can build up to a 5K race, which is just over 3 miles. And when you cross the finish line, you will feel like an Olympic champion ready to take on your next race! The point is that no one just decides to run a marathon the day of the race. It takes time to train and prepare your mind and body to run 26.2 miles. It starts by taking that first step and continuing to build up miles throughout each month from there. As you start that new project, job, business, church, idea, or venture, don't succumb to the pressure to skip steps because you feel you are somehow "behind" in comparison to everyone else. At the same time, don't let the overall goal overwhelm and paralyze you before you even get started. Rather, be intentional about following and completing the necessary steps one at a time.

Follow His leading

I find it so fascinating that you do not read in the text that the servants stopped to discuss what they were being instructed to do and what the possible consequences could be. They just followed Jesus' lead and obeyed His instructions. Can you imagine if Jesus had told *His disciples* to fill the stone jars with water and then draw some to give to the master of the banquet? They might have instructed Jesus to "send the crowd away" as they did when He was speaking to a crowd of five thousand people who were hungry. Just as the disciples did then, they probably would let Jesus know that it was "already very late" and that the guests could "go to the surrounding countryside and villages and buy themselves something to [drink]." And when He gave His disciples direction, they might have responded by letting Him know how many people were at the wedding banquet and how what they had was not going to be enough to serve everyone unless they went and bought more wine for all the guests and Philip would let Him know how much that would cost in a year's wages.

When Jesus gave the disciples instructions regarding feeding the crowd of five thousand, He was inviting the disciples to be part of a miracle; and they fought it every step of the way! They had already seen Jesus perform miracles, and they still had their own expectations on how things should happen. In stark contrast, the servants at the wedding did not know that they were being invited to be part of the first miracle that Jesus performed. They did not know who He was or what He could do. However, they did not give Him all the reasons it could not happen or suggest some other way to resolve the situation. They simply expected that Jesus was the one with the plan and He was going to be the one to provide the results. Oh, how I wish that I would consistently respond as the servants did when Jesus calls me to do something. Instead, I find myself often responding like the disciples and telling Jesus why something does not make sense or is not going to work. But the reality is, so often what God calls us to do does not make sense. We need to be open to following His lead and obeying His instructions. As we do that, we will experience the joy and deeper purpose of participating in what *He* is doing.

Keep walking by faith

For those who are followers of Christ, this journey is going to require walking by faith. I wish God would just give us a printout of His plan or how things are going to pan out in unknown seasons, but that's not His character or the type of relationship He wants to have with us. That would be like having robots who just follow instructions. The Lord wants to have a personal relationship with us. He wants us to grow in our faith and experience the fruit of that. It's what the servants at the wedding experienced when they engaged in what Jesus instructed them to do. It definitely was a literal walk of faith to approach the master of the banquet holding a cup that he expects has wine but you know you just poured water into! What's remarkable is we do not know when exactly the water turned into wine. It would be great if it was as the servants were pouring the water into the jars. Or if they were able to see the clear water turn red as they walked toward the master of the banquet. But what if the water did not change to wine until the cup was in the master's hands or touching his lips?

Recall that it was the servants who got to be a part of the first miracle Jesus performed. You and I also have the opportunity to be part of miracles that God wants to do. We just need to be open to following His lead, even when it doesn't make logical sense. I am cheering you on as you make a decision to walk by faith. Your knees may be trembling and your feet may feel unsteady, but just take one step at a time. He is right beside you and will never leave you. Together you will embark on the adventure of a lifetime. A journey so much more fulfilling than any sure-footed path would lead you on your own.

CHAPTER 8

A Needle, a Haystack, and a Guru

Spring is the season when entire landscapes come to life bursting with color. There is increased activity as animals awake from hibernation and birds return from their migration south. Nature's symphony stirs with the sounds of birds chirping, animals mating, others defending their territory, and babies being born. Snow is melting and flowers are opening up. Nature is ready to receive all that comes in the new season. In the same way, spring is a season for us to open our hearts to the new things God has for us and wants to do through us. Often it may not look as we envisioned but turns out to be exactly what we need. As we continue to grow toward the light of His Son, our hearts are transformed in His presence and we become more like Him.

"You're looking for a needle in a haystack." Those were the words of Dr. Neil Clark Warren, founder of eHarmony, after listening to me describe the man I was believing for. I didn't want to hear them. By age thirty, I had perfected my "list." It was four pages long, with double columns broken down into different categories. My list of requirements included character, spiritual, physical, and relational attributes. I had heard others tell me I was being too particular, but I figured they just lacked faith. Besides, it wasn't like the list contained unreasonable attributes. I made sure that everything I put on it was something that I lived up to as well. I had saved myself for marriage, so I expected he had, too. I was educated, physically fit, in leadership, financially independent, well-traveled, secure in my faith, and living out my purpose. Naturally, he needed to bring it as well!

As Dr. Warren listened to me ramble on about this ideal man, he asked, "Grace, do you trust me?" I replied, "Of course, you're Mr. eHarmony!" He said, "Grace, you're entering your thirties. Many men at your age have already been married, divorced, or had children." I frowned as I tried to focus on listening and being open to what this relationship guru was telling me. Normally, I would not let anyone rain on my parade and alter my stance of faith, but I felt that God was trying to get my attention. After all, the fact that I had even met Dr. Warren *and* that he offered to help me in this area that was causing me so much frustration was nothing short of a miracle. It was not something I'd asked for or sought out. We met during a chance morning workout. I normally did not stop to talk to strangers as I ran around the Rose Bowl. However, I recognized him as the man from the commercials who was encouraging people to try eHarmony. Even more so, I recognized him as an expert in the field of relationships, and I had a lot of questions I wanted to ask, so I introduced myself. After hearing some of my story, he offered to help however he could.

Only God could have arranged a meeting like that. I had so many blind spots that God had to bring a relationship guru to get some sense into me!

As much as I didn't like what Dr. Warren was saying, I knew our chance meeting was something God had orchestrated for that season in my life. And as much as everything in me wanted to state my case and give a rebuttal to what he was saying, I also recognized my approach was not working. I decided to open my heart to the counsel Dr. Warren generously shared, and we began to meet once a week while walking around the Rose Bowl. I read as many of his books as I could and came ready with questions to discuss.

He encouraged me to go on eHarmony.com. I resisted at first, but as I heard him share his heart and vision to connect people, I opened up to the idea. I was grateful for the opportunity to bring the list of my matches from eHarmony to get his thoughts and insight. I learned so much by seeing things through his eyes. I discovered I was measuring the matches, who were in their late twenties and early thirties, against men in my life whom I respected and admired—such as my dad, my pastor, and other elders in the church—who were in their fifties and sixties. I needed to realize that these men I looked up to had taken years to develop into who they were. I needed to be open to the fact that men my age would not currently be at that level of wisdom and maturity. Dr. Warren encouraged me not to lose hope but continue being open to meeting new people on eHarmony. He had such a conviction about this that he said as long as he was alive, I could be on eHarmony for free and that together we were going to find the man God had for me.

In this "spring" season of my journey, the Lord brought Dr. Warren into my life to help me open my heart and mind. In a move that could only be orchestrated by God, Dr. Warren took me under his wing as a spiritual daughter and spoke wisdom that would forever impact my life. Our walks continued for almost a year until he and his wife moved out of California. By the time of our last walk, my four-page list had been painfully edited down to ten Must Haves and ten Can't Stands (based on *Date or Soul Mate?*, by Neil Clark Warren, PhD). I was committed to being open to whomever God brought into my life whether or not he fit the picture I had previously had in my head.

To my single friends who are praying to get married, I know it may not look like anything is happening. There may not be any potential interests and the dating scene may look bleak. Just like a seed that is planted in the ground sees only darkness all around it, it's easy to look around and feel discouraged or alone. We can't see anything above the ground, and that creates a tendency, as we get older, to begin to worry that we are running out of time, that everyone is taken, and we are the only ones left who are single. I get it! There were days I was tempted to cross off everything I was believing for and just write, "Is he breathing?!?" But I want to encourage you that even though it does not seem like anything is happening, God is doing something. God has been working, God is working, and He will continue to work in your life. He knows what you need. He knows what you desire. He knows you better than you know yourself. You can trust Him.

A seed needs to be planted in the dirt for the process of growth to begin. In the darkness, it is lonely, it is isolated, and it doesn't feel like there is a purpose. The seed cannot see anything and cannot hear anything. From our perspective, it does not look like much is happening. But what we don't realize is that little seed is reaching toward the light. Note that it does not reach for other root systems; it does not try to see, copy, or compare what other seeds are doing. It does one thing: reach for the light. As it does, it begins to grow roots and to sprout. Each seed grows at its own pace, but none of them develop overnight. Likewise, as we keep reaching for the Son (aka Jesus), that's how we grow. That's how we walk through the unknown and unexpected seasons in life. That's how we stand through the winter storms. That's how we keep believing during the drought. That's how we can be at peace in the waiting. We keep reaching toward the Son of God. Our new prayer becomes, *Lord, I just want to be with you.*

Draw me close to you. Mature trees will bend in the direction of the strongest light and grow more branches on the side of the tree that is exposed to more light. As we follow Christ, His light leads us, so we don't get lost in the dark. It nourishes us, provides wisdom, and guides us along our path.

It reminds me of a science experiment that is often done in elementary school. Students plant a seed in two different pots. One pot is placed by a window to receive natural light and the other is put in a box, closet, or some other dark space. At first there seems to be no difference in the plants as they sprout. However, the one in the dark soon becomes pale and thin while the one in the light flourishes as it turns its leaves to the sun. In the same way, what we are growing toward makes a difference in whether we flourish or wither. Jesus said, "I am the light of the world. Whoever follows me will never walk in darkness, but will have the light of life" (John 8:12 NIV). Through social media, we have the ability to follow hundreds and thousands of people. Nothing wrong with that. I just want to encourage you that the person you want to follow the most closely is Jesus. The one you want to search for each day and see what they are doing in the world is Jesus. The one you want to be listening for and have notifications to alert you whenever He says anything is Jesus. We need to be careful that all the people we are following do not distract us from seeing and following the light from the One we truly need to follow.

The Lord used Neil Clark Warren to open my heart (and mind!) to be able to receive what He had for me. To be open to the fact that my future husband may not look like I had envisioned. But while I was a hot mess and needed a lot of work to open my heart to something that did not fit my preconceived notions, I don't believe that's the main challenge most people face. The real obstacles come when you have previously opened your heart to someone and it got stabbed, betrayed, or shredded. How do you once again be open to engage in new friendships or relationships? In the fall season, we focused on opening our hearts to let go of past hurts and offenses. The spring season now focuses on opening our hearts to *receive* what God has for us. Because we did the work of releasing things that could potentially hold us back, we are now able to receive new things.

Maybe your heart was so deeply hurt that you don't know how you can ever open it again. You forgave them, but you do not intend to put yourself in a position to be hurt again. You don't know how you can ever trust again after the betrayal of that colleague, family member, or partner. You thought they were for you and had your best interest in mind. You opened your heart to them and they trampled all over it. So you made the decision:

> I'm never going to trust another person.
> I'm not going to rely on anyone again.
> I'm not letting anyone else in.
> I've got to look out for me.
> Never again will I let someone in and be hurt like that.

I hear you. I wish you had never experienced that betrayal, attack, or humiliation. It makes total sense why everything in you wants to shut everyone else out and not open up to new relationships. But that's not how you are meant to live. There is so much more God has for your life. He wants you to flourish. I want you to flourish. And I'm sure that's what you want, too. As comforting as it is to put up walls around your heart, you know you were not designed that way. You were created for more than that. You were designed to live and experience all that God has for you! Your heart can feel free and light with the wonder of a child. You can be fully present and at peace even in the midst of unknown and unexpected seasons in life.

So how exactly does that happen? How do you open your heart

after experiencing pain, disappointment, and hurt? How do you trust again and believe the best in people? Everything in you wants to take your heart and lock it in a safe, shielded far from any potential attacks. And while that might provide some protection, it is also the very thing that will prevent us from flourishing. There's a rising leader who discovered just that when his character was smeared and his life was in danger. From a young age, David knew he was going to do great things. A prophet had spoken over his life that he would be king. However, the path to the palace did not go as he had envisioned. It was filled with unknown and unexpected twists and turns. David went from tending his father's sheep to becoming one of King Saul's armor bearers and playing the harp for him. While still going back and forth between serving the king and taking care of the household sheep, David took on and defeated Goliath, the imposing warrior from the enemy's army. David's victory brought freedom to the Israelites and prompted the women from "all the towns of Israel" to dance and sing, "Saul has slain his thousands and David his tens of thousands" (1 Samuel 18:7 NIV). This resulted in King Saul attempting to kill David three times as his jealousy escalated to another level. David fled, and King Saul pursued him with his army. It is there that we find the would-be king in a cave dodging spears to his heart. And in that space of heartache and betrayal, David did not kill Saul when he had the opportunity. He knew that throwing a spear and retaliating was not part of his purpose. Instead, we know from the psalms he wrote that David turned toward the light of the Son and worshipped the Lord.

It's been said that we should aim to "live a life that demands an explanation." When we choose to open our hearts again after an offense or a deep wound, we are doing just that. When we make the decision to trust God and praise Him in the midst of the pain and heartache, we are doing that. The world would say, "You better watch your back. You can't trust anyone. You're the only one who can look out for yourself." But we are talking about opening our hearts for Christ's love to shine through. As followers of Christ whose hearts have been transformed by Jesus, I believe we have the opportunity to respond to situations differently, in a way that causes people to ask, "What's up with that? Why does she have peace when the world is going crazy? How can he love that person after what he has gone through?" I'm trying to live a life where Jesus is the hero of my story.

Several years ago, I got an unexpected phone call from my mom. In short and belabored sentences, she said her chest felt tight and she was having trouble breathing. Before she could finish describing how she felt very weak, cold, and clammy, I told her she needed to get to the hospital right away. I rushed from my office and flew down the highway to the hospital emergency room. As I had suspected, Mom was having a heart attack. Everything was a blur as I tried to get details, see how she was doing, get clearance, understand what the medical staff was saying, and determine when to contact the rest of the family. I had somehow managed to call one of my sisters as soon as I had hung up with Mom. As we waited for other family members and friends to arrive, we learned that the doctors were taking Mom into surgery and putting a stent in her artery that was blocked. It was a nerve-wracking few hours. Thankfully, the procedure went smoothly, and Mom recovered well.

I hope you don't ever have to receive such a phone call or go through such a traumatic experience. So why did I bring it up? Stay with me for a moment, and it will all make sense. I first want to give a little context to make sure we're all on the same page when it comes to what exactly a heart attack is and what causes it. When blood flow is severely reduced or cut off to the heart, a heart attack happens, and the heart muscle begins to die. If blood flow isn't restored quickly, a heart attack can cause permanent heart damage and death. Doctors put a tiny tube called a stent in the artery to keep it open and prevent it from narrowing or closing again.

Why all the medical talk? I believe some of us need to get a *spiritual* heart stent to open up our arteries and bring life to our hearts. Over the years, plaque has accumulated from past hurts, disappointments, and pain. Each time you vowed never to trust anyone again, not to let anyone in close, or not to reveal your authentic self, another layer was added that hardened the arteries leading to your heart. And just like there are often no warning signs that the arteries are closing and the heart is slowly dying, we may not realize our spiritual heart is becoming hard. But it does not need to stay that way. The Lord promises in Ezekiel 36:26, "I will give you a new heart and put a new spirit in you; I will remove from you your heart of stone and give you a heart of flesh" (NIV). However, it is not something that He forces to make happen; it's something we need to pursue just like King David did when he cried out to the Lord, "Create in me a pure heart, O God, and renew a steadfast spirit within me" (Psalm 51:10 NIV). We all desire to flourish in life. I can't think of anyone who has said their goal is to wither. We want to grow, thrive, prosper, and live a fulfilling life. One of the things that impacts how or if we walk in our purpose is the condition of our heart. A closed heart is going to have a very difficult time trying to flourish in life. Let us follow David's example and ask the Lord to create in us a pure heart that His love can flow through.

Sometimes the pain from a personal attack is so powerful that, although you have forgiven, it has the power to derail you and keep you from flourishing. Their salacious words and actions still echo in your head, like a poison poured into the soil where you are planted. Your roots slowly begin to absorb the poison and carry it throughout the trunk, branches, and leaves of the tree. And as each cell absorbs the liquid as truth, the tree slowly begins to die. In such depths of heartache, like a seed planted in the soil, I find myself looking upward toward the sun. Jesus is the light that our broken hearts need. There is no other source that is able to bring healing and restoration. No one else has the antidote for the poison of offense. Staying in the dark holding on to wounds will cause us to wither and forgo our purpose. We are not able to flourish in such a space. Instead, we have been wired to seek the light. To be in the Lord's presence. There is nothing humankind has created that can come close to that. We can come just as we are. He is not looking for us to be perfect before we draw closer to Him. He just wants us to be with Him. As we stay in His presence, we are made whole.

When I am having a hard time opening my heart to express love again, there's a story that helps me recalibrate. Long before Jesus hung on the cross—in fact, just before he was starting His public ministry—Jesus was almost canceled. Can you *imagine* that? For those of you who are having a hard time believing it, I'll show it to you. But first let me give you some context.

After Jesus had spent forty days in the wilderness being tempted by the devil, He emerged in the power of the Spirit and began teaching in synagogues in Galilee and Nazareth. Everyone praised Him and was amazed by His gracious words. All spoke well of Him…that is, until He said something they found offensive. "All the people in the synagogue were furious," and things suddenly shifted. "They got up, drove him out of the town, and took him to the brow of the hill on which the town was built, *in order to throw him off the cliff.* But he walked right through the crowd and went on his way" Luke 4:28–30 (NIV, emphasis added).

While I have had people say some horrible things and dismiss me, I have never had a crowd of people try to kill me. Hopefully you and I will never experience anything like that. While we may not know what it's like to have a group of people try and throw us off a cliff physically, I imagine some of us have experienced something similar in a relationship that went toxic. If you haven't, I'm genuinely happy for you. However, I would encourage you to still learn from this story, because if you are breathing, chances are this will be useful in the future.

If one of the first responses to me stepping out in my purpose resulted in almost getting killed before I could get things off the ground, I probably would have been reconsidering my calling. Maybe looking into other things that were not as public, but rather behind the scenes. Something that would allow me to live long enough to fulfill my mission *while* enjoying my life. And of course, I would be hurt and angry for days. In case you missed it, this took place when Jesus had gone back to Nazareth, where He was brought up. I would be so upset and ready to throw punches. How could my own people treat me like that? However, that is not what Jesus did. The key thing I learned from Jesus in this passage is that He did not let the words or actions of others get to Him and throw Him off course. It says that He "walked right through the crowd and went on his way." In other words, He stayed on mission. He did not stop and try to explain Himself or help them see they had a wrong image of Him. Nor did He get stuck brooding over what had been said about Him. He did not get offended, angry, hurt, or depressed. He simply went on His way. If they were not going to listen to Him or receive His message, He was moving on to others who would. He stayed on mission!

My friend, in order to flourish, in order to be open to the things God has for you and the things He wants to do in your life, you cannot let the vile words and actions of others throw you off course. It's important to note that this near-death experience happened shortly after Jesus came out of the wilderness, where He had been tempted by the devil for forty days. The Bible tells us that Jesus entered that space "full" of the Holy Spirit (see Luke 4:1). When he emerged, it was "in the power" of the Holy Spirit. The transformation that occurred allowed Jesus to walk through such an attack unscathed. What that tells me is we need to be filled with the Holy Spirit. That's what Paul encouraged in his letter to the saints in Ephesus, when he said to "be filled with the Spirit" (Ephesians 5:18 NIV). It's the same for all of us today. We need to pray for the Holy Spirit to fill us and guide us daily.

As we've seen, before Jesus started His public ministry, He spent forty days in the wilderness being tempted by the devil. But did you know that *after* Jesus had completed His mission, after He had taken on the sin of the world, died, and risen again, He remained on earth for another *forty* days? If you did not realize that, you may be wondering what exactly was He doing? After all, if I had just hung on a cross, taken on the sin of the world, and the people I had mentored for three years had deserted me, I would've been, like, "Peace out, I did what the Father told me to do and I'm going back to be with Him!"

But after three years of public ministry, after enduring unimaginable suffering, and after completing what He was sent to do, why would Jesus linger for another forty days? Each of the Gospels give us snapshots of whom Jesus appeared to and some of what He said. But I want to focus on what Luke tells us in Acts 1:3. He writes, "After his suffering, [Jesus] presented himself to [the apostles] and gave many convincing proofs that he was alive. He appeared to them over a period of forty days and spoke about the kingdom of God" (NIV). I think we all need to pause for a moment and let it sink in that Jesus was talking about the Kingdom of God and *not* what He had just been through.

Unbelievable! In our culture today, if someone gets our order wrong or says or does something we don't agree with, we make sure people know about it. Jesus had just been betrayed and defeated the enemy, sin, and death, but did not talk about any of that. He spoke about the Kingdom of God. There is so much to learn from that, but I want to focus on one of the final things He said before ascending into heaven at the end of those forty days. He said, "You will receive power when the Holy Spirit comes on you; and you will be my witnesses in Jerusalem, and in all Judea and Samaria, and to the ends of the earth" (Acts 1:8 NIV). Jesus was telling us that we need to be filled with the power of the Holy Spirit just like He was. That, my friends, is the only way that we will be able to keep our spiritual "stent" open. Without asking the Holy Spirit to fill and empower us daily—and sometimes moment by moment—we run the danger of our heart being blocked. Just like fat and cholesterol, resentment and offense easily adhere to the walls of our arteries and block the flow of love in and out of our hearts. As we rely on the power of the Holy Spirit like Jesus did, we will be able to keep our hearts open, stay on mission, and fulfill all that the Lord has called us to do. And what is our mission? When one of the expert teachers of the law asked Jesus what the most important commandment is, Jesus replied: "'Love the Lord your God with all your heart and with all your soul and with all your mind and with all your strength.' The second is this: 'Love your neighbor as yourself.' There is no commandment greater than these" (Mark 12: 30–31 NIV).

I find it remarkable that Jesus walked with the very person who would betray Him. After giving a teaching that the Jews and his disciples found hard to receive, Jesus said, "'The words I have spoken to you—they are full of the Spirit and life. Yet there are some of you who do not believe.' For Jesus had known from the beginning which of them did not believe and who would betray him" (John 6:63b–64 NIV). This shows us that Jesus knew for about three years that Judas would be the one to betray Him. For three years they journeyed together, they did life together, and they were a key part of each other's lives. Jesus not only invited Judas to be part of His mission, but He gave him authority to heal every disease and sickness, preach, drive out demons, and build the Kingdom. Most of us are not aware of when a person is going to betray us. And if we do get an idea that betrayal might happen, we are quick to cut the person off. But who knowingly invites a future traitor to be in their inner circle? Honestly my mind cannot even comprehend that. I don't think I will ever be at that level of spiritual maturity. But let's put that on the shelf for now and take things back to the beginning of their relationship to see what we can learn.

Matthew, Mark, and Luke each give accounts of when Judas Iscariot was first invited to be a disciple, but I think it's hilarious how Luke lets it be known up front that Judas became a traitor. Just in case there was any confusion about which of the twelve it was that betrayed Jesus.

"One of those days Jesus went out to a mountainside to pray, and spent the night praying to God. When morning came, he called his disciples to him and chose twelve of them, whom he also designated apostles: Simon (whom he named Peter), his brother Andrew, James, John, Philip, Bartholomew, Matthew, Thomas, James son of Alphaeus, Simon who was called the Zealot, Judas son of James, and **Judas Iscariot, who became a traitor**" (Luke 6:12–16 NIV, emphasis added).

What's also interesting to point out is that according to this passage, Jesus extended the invitation to Judas and the others after He had spent the night praying on a mountainside. In other words, He was not making a rash decision. He had spent hours in prayer seeking the Lord's will. And somehow Judas was part of the plan. I mention that for a couple reasons. First, all betrayal is incredibly painful, but it's one thing when it's someone who does not know you that well versus someone who has been in your inner circle for years. It would have been painful for Jesus to have been betrayed by one of the priests or someone He'd healed on His journey. It's a whole other level of pain for it to have been one of the twelve who were with Him on almost a daily basis. It can sometimes feel like there should be a special place in hell for those who turn on us after all we have poured into them, sacrificed for them, and given ourselves to be part of a greater mission together. And yet Jesus still invited Judas, knowing the pain he would inflict. The second reason I mention this is because Jesus extended the invitation to Judas after an all-night prayer meeting. I don't know about you, but if I had spent all night praying to God, I would envision that whatever He spoke or directed me to do was not going to result in a traitor being in my midst. Under no circumstance would I see that as part of the plan. The purpose of me going to prayer in the first place is to receive wisdom on how to proceed and avoid such painful situations. I cannot tell you how many times I've said, or heard others say: "I prayed and that____ still happened," or "I prayed and that ____ didn't happen." My friend, if there's one thing I've learned after being on this faith journey for over forty years, it's that what the Lord told the prophet Isaiah is still true: "For My thoughts *are* not your thoughts, Nor *are* your ways My ways," says the LORD. "For *as* the heavens are higher than the earth, So are My ways higher than your ways, And My thoughts than your thoughts" (Isaiah 55:8–9 NKJV).

After a few years, things shifted in Judas and he "went to the chief priests and the officers of the temple guard and discussed with them how he might betray Jesus. They were delighted and agreed to give him money. He consented, and watched for an opportunity to hand Jesus over to them when no crowd was present" (Luke 22:4–6 NIV). Sometimes in life it can seem like the haters are just watching and waiting for an opportunity to pounce. It has been my experience that they often strike during the spring and summer seasons when things are shifting for the better in your life. They had no problem when you were letting go of things during the fall or just trying to stand during your winter season. But when God begins to move, when He begins to bless you or you receive the answer to your prayers, watch out for those who will want to cut you down. They have no idea how long, how lonely, and how painful your winter season was. All they see is you getting something "you don't deserve." I'm just letting you know, because I had no idea that the Lord's favor and blessing would draw haters out of the woodwork. But what are we going to do when that happens? We're going to do like Jesus did and keep our hearts clean and stay on mission!

Jesus' mission was to do the will of the Father. Jesus said, "For I have come down from heaven not to do my will but to do the will of him who sent me" (John 6:38 NIV). "My food is to do the will of him who sent me and to accomplish his work" (John 4:34 ESV). "I do nothing on my own but speak just what the Father has taught me. The one who sent me is with me; he has not left me alone, for I always do what pleases him" (John 8:28–29 NIV). As followers of Christ, our mission, like Jesus, is to do the will of the Father. We need to be open to the fact that it often does not look like we envisioned or would have planned. We can see the anguish that Jesus experienced in His last meal with His disciples.

"After he had said this, Jesus was troubled in spirit and testified, 'Very truly I tell you, one of you is going to betray me.'" His disciples stared at one another, at a loss to know which of them he meant. One of them, the disciple whom Jesus loved, was reclining next to him. Simon Peter motioned to this disciple and said, "Ask him which one he means." Leaning back against Jesus, John asked Him, "Lord, who is it?" Jesus answered, "It is the one to whom I will give this piece of bread when I have dipped it in the dish." Then, dipping the piece of bread, he gave it to Judas, the son of Simon Iscariot. As soon as Judas took the bread, Satan entered into him. So Jesus told him, "What you are about to do, do quickly" (John 13:21–27 NIV).

Jesus could have dipped the bread into poison. He could have had angels strike Judas down or done any number of things to stop him. However, Jesus had submitted to the Father's will. Even as He would pray a short time later in Gethsemane, "Father, if you are willing, take this cup from me," His obedience and complete surrender was evident as He immediately followed His request with "yet not my will, but yours be done" (Luke 22:42 NIV).

After praying for the third time, "My Father, if it is not possible for this cup to be taken away unless I drink it, may your will be done" (Matthew 26:42 NIV), Jesus "returned to the disciples and said to them, 'Are you still sleeping and resting? Look, the hour has come, and the Son of Man is delivered into the hands of sinners. Rise! Let us go! Here comes my betrayer!' While he was still speaking, Judas, one of the Twelve, arrived. With him was a large crowd armed with swords and clubs, sent from the chief priests and the elders of the people. Now the betrayer had arranged a signal with them: 'The one I kiss is the man; arrest him.' Going at once to Jesus, Judas said, 'Greetings, Rabbi!' and kissed him. Jesus replied, 'Do what you came for, **friend**'"(Matthew 26: 45–50 NIV).

And there it is. The most amazing example of an open heart. Jesus literally called his betrayer "friend." I was undone when I first saw that. I literally had to look it up in Greek to make sure the Bible translators had not made a mistake. To me, Judas is synonymous with traitor. His face is right there in the dictionary instead of a definition. As well as the other people who have done me wrong in the past or are currently getting on my last nerve. But when Jesus addressed Judas, He called him friend.

I'll just let that sit for a minute.

Before we close this chapter, I want to point out one more remarkable thing about Jesus. Despite all the malicious things that were said about Him, to Him, and done to Him, Jesus did not rant to His disciples, the crowd of followers, or anyone else about what happened;

He spoke to the Father. He did not post a picture of Judas on social media with #traitor, nor did He let everyone know that Nazareth was not the place to go visit because they tried to kill Him. He did not get together with His small group (aka the disciples) and say, "Can you believe what they did to Me? How dare they say that about Me." In those instances and many others, He just continued to talk (aka pray) to the Father. It has been said that Jesus' ministry involved going from one place of prayer to another. And in between He healed people, talked about the Kingdom, and set people free. That's how I want to live my life. Growing toward the Son, spending time in His presence, and becoming more like Him each day. Opening my heart to whatever He wants to do in and through me. Having ongoing conversations with the Lord and living out His purpose for my life. That, my friends, is how we truly flourish.

CHAPTER 9

Blank Sheets of Paper

When I first started looking for a house back when I was single, at the top of my list of must-haves was a view. I wanted to be able to wake up, open my eyes, and see the beauty of California, whether it was the ocean, the mountains, or the valleys. I had fallen in love with the stunning view from the home my family moved into when I was in high school. Located on the San Gabriel Mountains, it had an incredible view of the valley. On July Fourth, we could see numerous fireworks shows taking place in the surrounding cities. As I began to search for my own place, I focused on the foothill cities in the hopes of finding a home with a similar view. City after city had beautiful Spanish-style homes with breathtaking views. However, my dream burst as I realized most of the properties were well out of my price range. As reality set in, I began to get discouraged, confused as to why God was not "giving me the desires of my heart." It had been just over five years since I had given all the money for my down payment to the church. Once again, I had rigorously saved my money, sacrificed, and gone without for so long. I had prayed, fasted, and believed, but was still short several zeros of what I needed to get into my dream home.

I came to my senses and embraced the reality that my first home was not going to be my dream home. I realized I needed a different approach if I wanted to get my own place. I started with what I enjoy doing best: I created a list, of course! I wrote down the places I spent most of my time outside of work. They included the gym, Trader Joe's, and a handful of favorite shops and restaurants. I got a paper map (yes, such things used to exist) and drew a large circle centered around the city I worked in. It represented the distance I was willing to drive to get to work. If you've been to LA, you know traffic is absolutely brutal. And for those who live there, it is a key factor in determining your daily routine or how much you are willing to endure for a night out. After drawing a radius that represented an hour-long commute, I then circled all the locations of my gym that were within the bearable driving distance. I did the same in a different color for Trader Joe's, favorite restaurants, and shopping centers. There were a few cities that had all three colored circles. That's where I chose to focus my search.

After looking at more houses than I could count within my range, I remember seeing a listing for a three-bedroom, two-bath, Spanish-style home. I initially wrote it off because the garage was the prominent feature in the pictures of the front of the home. But since I wanted to live in that particular city, I added it to my list of viewings to get to know the area. My friend and I made what I thought was going to be a quick walk through the property, fully intending to move on to others on my list with more curb appeal. But when we walked into the empty home, I experienced something I had not felt in any of the other properties I had seen. The commotion and busyness of the day stood still. The sounds of cars driving and kids playing all dwindled. My realtor and I stood still. We both felt it. Something so precious and priceless. Peace. I took a deep breath in and exhaled slowly. No other home had felt so calm right when I walked in the door. As I stood in the entryway, without having seen the rest of the home, I knew this was the one. After viewing the entire property, I told my agent I wanted to make an offer. I was so excited that I had found my home. However, my hopes were once again crushed when I found out someone had made an all-cash offer. Although housing prices had dropped, I could not understand why anyone with that type of money would be impinging on "my" home. I tried looking at other properties, but I just couldn't get it out of my mind. At the same time, it didn't look possible.

I prayed.

Nothing changed.

I fasted.

Nothing changed.

I cried out to God and had close friends join me in believing for a miracle.

Weeks went by and nothing changed. So with a heavy heart, I moved on.

Then several months later my agent called me out of the blue and asked if I was still interested in the home. "Of course!" I responded emphatically. "What happened? I thought they had a cash buyer?"

She said that the buyer had rescinded the offer and decided to go with a different property.

I eventually got the home and had the biggest house-warming party to celebrate what God had done!

The process of buying my first home was very emotional and draining. However, it taught me a life-changing principle. God knows what we need better than we do. I thought I needed a house with a view because that's what I had grown up with and had come to enjoy. The house God blessed me with did not have the number one thing on my list: a view. Instead it had the number one thing on God's list: a safe haven. The house was one of only two homes on a quiet cul-de-sac in a peaceful community. My neighbor was an older single woman who had lived there for years and took meticulous care of her home. I did not know that having a peaceful place to come home to was actually far more important than a view or anything else on my list.

I now have a better understanding of what the Lord means in Isaiah 55:8–9: "'For my thoughts are not your thoughts, neither are your ways my ways,' declares the Lord. 'As the heavens are higher than the earth, so are my ways higher than your ways and my thoughts than your thoughts'" (NIV). God knew that as an introvert who worked at a church thousands of people visited every weekend, I needed a peaceful safe haven to come home to. Can I encourage you in whatever you are waiting and believing the Lord for? He knows what you really need. You can trust Him and His timing. He knows you better than you know yourself. He knows your past, your present, and your future. He knows what and who you need in your life to truly flourish. Allow Him to lead you and guide your steps. When you find yourself doubting His direction or questioning His timing, it might help to think of this: There is no one who would hike Mt. Everest or Mt. Kilimanjaro without a sherpa, guide, or guiding company. In fact, it is required for these climbs. As a first-time climber, you gladly place your life in the hands of a complete stranger! You trust them completely because they have made the climb successfully. They know the mountain, the path to take, where to rest, what gear to pack, and how to physically and mentally prepare. Can I submit to you that the God who created the entire universe, who created the mountains, and who knows all things, is offering to lead you and guide you?! What are you waiting for?! Why are you doubting Him? There is no one better you can trust! He knows every path on every mountain you are facing today. Know that His ways are higher than our ways and His thoughts are higher than our thoughts. I would much rather follow His thoughts and ways than attempt to climb the mountain on my own.

Soon after this experience, I decided to get rid of all my "lists," including the one for my future husband. I gave the Lord a blank piece of paper to write His list for the man He had for me. I trusted that just as God knew what I needed in a home, He also knew what I needed in a husband. I know it can be a little scary to give the Lord a blank sheet of paper. *What if He writes something that I am not comfortable with? What if He writes something that does not make logical sense?* Yes, there will be plenty of things that stretch us out of our comfort zone and do not make sense to our minds, but it is the greatest adventure. One day walking in the unknown and unexpected *with God* is so much more fulfilling than a lifetime that is known and planned without Him. One invites you to a deep relationship, a greater level of trust, and the opportunity to be part of something so much bigger than yourself. To live out a purpose that will outlast you. I want to encourage you to be open to God's direction and His will. He is the author of this grand story. He knows you better than you know yourself. "I am certain that God, who began the good work within you, will continue his work until it is finally finished on the day when Christ Jesus returns" (Philippians 1:6 NLT). I don't want anything in me to block what He wants to do in and through me. I have learned through my own experiences and those of others that it's just not worth it.

Paul writes in 2 Corinthians 3:3, "You show that you are a letter from Christ, the result of our ministry, written not with ink but with the Spirit of the living God, not on tablets of stone but on tablets of human hearts" (NIV). That is how I want to live my life. As a blank tablet for the Lord to write *His* story. I'm done with all my "lists." Instead, I offer my life, my heart, and all its desires to the Lord. I have seen and experienced how He knows me and what I need much more than I do. I simply say, "Lord, You have my life, You have my heart, You have all of me. Have Your way, Lord. Like a blank sheet of paper, I give You my heart. Write *Your* story on my heart that I might reflect

Your love in this world. Let Your love flow through me in such a way that draws people to You. May my life shine for You. Write what You want said to a world that is so broken, worn down, confused, and hurting. Holy Spirit, write the character of Jesus into my inmost being that I may carry Your sweet aroma wherever I go."

There's a well-known story in the Bible that illustrates the additional challenges we can bring upon ourselves when we insist on doing things our own way instead of embracing what God is doing. The story tells how the Israelites wandered about in the wilderness for forty years before reaching the promised land. This journey would have normally taken eleven days. I've heard people teach that it took the Israelites so long because they grumbled and complained, and God punished them. And while they did a lot of grumbling and complaining, that was not the reason that they wandered for forty years. I hope that when you look at what really caused the delay, it will impact how you view future unknown and unexpected circumstances. But first, let's set some context.

In Genesis 12:1–5, God tells Abram, "'Go from your country, your people and your father's household to the land I will show you. I will make you into a great nation.'…So Abram went.…they set out for the land of Canaan, and they arrived there" (NIV). In Canaan, we see the generations of Abraham, Isaac, Jacob, and Joseph. Joseph was sold by his brothers and taken to Egypt. After enduring a false accusation, prison, and other trials, God used him to interpret Pharaoh's dream. Because of the wisdom from the dream, Joseph was able to prepare Egypt for the famine that was coming. Pharaoh, King of Egypt, said to Joseph, "I hereby put you in charge of the whole land of Egypt"(Genesis 41:41 NIV). During the famine, Joseph's brothers came to buy food. Once he revealed to them who he was and assured them that he had forgiven them, Joseph had his whole family move to Egypt, where they flourished and grew in number.

Exodus 1:6–11 tells of a key change of events:

> Now Joseph and all his brothers and all that generation died, but the Israelites were exceedingly fruitful; they multiplied greatly, increased in numbers and became so numerous that the land was filled with them. Then a new king, to whom Joseph meant nothing, came to power in Egypt. "Look," he said to his people, "the Israelites have become far too numerous for us. Come, we must deal shrewdly with them or they will become even more numerous and, if war breaks out, will join our enemies, fight against us and leave the country." So, they put slave masters over them to oppress them with forced labor. (NIV)

The Israelite population had grown so large that the Egyptians were concerned they could be overpowered. So they made the Israelites slaves, and that lasted for 430 years until Moses was raised up to deliver them and take them back to the promised land (see Exodus 12:40). The Lord delivered the Israelites from the Egyptians with mighty signs and wonders. The miracles continued as they crossed the Red Sea and entered the desert. At one point the Lord told Moses, "Send some men to explore the land of Canaan, which I am giving to the Israelites" (Numbers 13:2 NIV). Twelve men went and explored the land for forty days. They reported that the land flowed with milk and honey, but the people were powerful and the cities were fortified. One of the twelve, Caleb, said, "'We should go up and take possession of the land, for we can certainly do it'" (Numbers 13:30 NIV), but the rest of the men said, "'We can't attack those people; they are stronger than we are.' And they spread among the Israelites a bad report about the land they had explored" (Numbers 13:31–32 NIV).

The next thing you know, all the Israelites were grumbling against

Moses and Aaron and wishing for another leader who would take them back to Egypt. To Egypt! Where they had endured centuries of bondage. Caleb and Joshua, two of the twelve men who had explored the land, both "tore their clothes and said to the entire Israelite assembly, 'The land we passed through and explored is exceedingly good. If the LORD is pleased with us, he will lead us into that land, a land flowing with milk and honey, and will give it to us. Only do not rebel against the LORD. And do not be afraid of the people of the land, because we will devour them. Their protection is gone, but the LORD is with us. Do not be afraid of them'" (Numbers 14:6–9 NIV). But in response to their passionate plea, the whole assembly wanted to stone Joshua and Caleb.

It is against this backdrop that the Lord said to Moses and Aaron:

"How long will this wicked community grumble against me? I have heard the complaints of these grumbling Israelites. So tell them, 'As surely as I live, declares the LORD, I will do to you the very thing I heard you say: In this wilderness your bodies will fall—every one of you twenty years old or more who was counted in the census and who has grumbled against me. Not one of you will enter the land I swore with uplifted hand to make your home, except Caleb son of Jephunneh and Joshua son of Nun. As for your children that you said would be taken as plunder, I will bring them in to enjoy the land you have rejected. But as for you, your bodies will fall in this wilderness. Your children will be shepherds here for forty years, suffering for your unfaithfulness, until the last of your bodies lies in the wilderness. **For forty years—one year for each of the forty days you explored the land—you will suffer for your sins and know what it is like to have me against you.'** I, the LORD, have spoken, and I will surely do these things to this whole wicked community, which has banded together against me. They will meet their end in this wilderness; here they will die." (Numbers 14:27–35 NIV, emphasis added)

Did you catch that? The Lord was displeased with how the Israelites responded to the promised land He was bringing them to. Instead of walking into the land that He had already given them, they chose to cower in fear and wish for the old days in Egypt…where they were in captivity. So the Israelites spent forty years wandering around in the wilderness. One year for each day they had explored the land the Lord had given them and believed a negative report.

There is so much to glean from this story. The fact that God is always working. The fact that our lives are part of a larger story. The importance of believing in His Word and His promises. How God desires to be with us…I could go on and on. The main takeaway I want us to get from this story is a desire to see things as the Lord sees them. The lack of that is really what caused things to go sideways in this story. Joshua and Caleb were the only two spies who saw things as the Lord did. Yes, they saw in the natural what the other ten spies saw; but they did not stop there. They saw in the spiritual that the Lord was with them and had already given them the land. The other spies did not see that. They saw giants, powerful people, and fortified cities. God had just delivered the Israelites from Egypt with never-before-seen miracles. And after that, the ten spies were able to convince all the Israelites to see the challenges they saw, instead of the blessing God had promised them. As a result, all of Israel saw the promised land as a problem that was bigger than their God. They grumbled, complained, and started looking for a leader to take them back to Egypt. But not Joshua and Caleb. They believed and tried to convince the people that although there were giants, the

Lord was bigger than the giants. He would give them the land as He promised.

I do not know what you are facing right now. It may feel overwhelming, with no way through or around it. Stepping out in that new business venture, going back to school, raising kids on your own after a divorce, believing again after disappointment, buying a home by yourself, taking care of an aging parent—they all may seem daunting. Like the spies, you might feel like little grasshoppers in the eyes of giants. But I want to encourage you to see God as bigger than that situation. God gets the glory as we trust Him with whatever we are facing. The bigger your challenge, the more opportunity there is for God to be glorified as you trust Him with it.

Write down whatever situation or challenge you are facing today:

....

Now write the words "God is bigger than" in front of the thing you wrote:

....

When things get overwhelming or challenging, one of the things I like to pray is "Lord, help me to see what You see in this situation. Help me to see what You see in this person." He might show you their brokenness or insecurity. Not for you to point out to them or others. But for you to have compassion and understanding and to pray for them. He might show you that when they are acting out, it does not have anything to do with you, but rather their own issues and wounds that have been triggered. He might show you that there is more to the situation than you see with your natural eyes. That there is a spiritual battle taking place and you need to open your eyes, get suited up, and get ready to face the real enemy. We can only see a limited perspective with our natural eyes. One of many stories that illustrate that involves a king in the Old Testament who was angry with the prophet Elisha. When the King of Aram sent a strong force with horses and chariots to surround the city that Elisha was in, his servant was alarmed. Elisha saw past what was a threat in the natural. He saw what God saw in the spiritual and calmly told his servant, "'Don't be afraid.... Those who are with us are more than those who are with them.' And Elisha prayed, 'Open his eyes, LORD, so that he may see.' Then the LORD opened the servant's eyes, and he looked and saw the hills full of horses and chariots of fire all around Elisha" (2 Kings 6:16–17 NIV).

When we see only in the natural, we miss out on what God is doing in the spiritual. Over the years, I have learned to ask the Lord to open my eyes. Open my eyes to see in the spiritual, not just the natural. Open my eyes to see people like you do. Open my eyes to see this situation like you do. When we see only in the natural, we get confused as to who our real enemy is. We get distracted by fighting the wrong battles. It's one of the enemy's tactics to throw us off course. But Ephesians 6:12 admonishes us, "For we are not fighting against flesh-and-blood enemies, but against evil rulers and authorities of the unseen world, against mighty powers in this dark world, and against evil spirits in the heavenly places" (NLT).

It reminds me of a cardinal that was incessantly pecking at one of our bathroom windows starting just after 5:00 a.m. each morning. Like many birds, cardinals mate and give birth in the spring. They are very territorial birds, and once they claim a home area, they will protect it by chasing away other birds. When they see another cardinal in their breeding or feeding territory, they instinctively attack the other bird. Unfortunately, windows act as mirrors to the birds. When they see their reflection, they interpret this as an intruder and begin attacking or pecking at the window to chase the intruder away. This particular spring, the window in our master bathroom was the mirror and that cardinal put up a fight every day. As soon as the sun started to come up, we were awoken by its vigorous attack against the "other bird." We researched the internet and tried just about every suggestion mentioned to get cardinals to stop pecking at windows. Because the window was too high for us to reach from outside, we could only make adjustments from the inside. We put up strips of ribbon on the window, but the bird still kept relentlessly pecking. We put up pictures of owls and other bigger birds, and while it seemed to work temporarily, the cardinal decided it was going to take on the larger predators! It just would not stop fighting its reflection, all day every day. The reality is that once a bird realizes it can see its reflection in the window, it's going to return to that place and continue attacking again and again. And while that seems so ridiculous to us, the reality is that we often get caught up doing the same thing.

Something happens at work or at home, and we get tangled up in the situation. We begin to obsess over what the coworker or family member said or did. Just like the cardinal, instead of living out our purpose, our focus and energy turn to retaliation. All of heaven tries to tell us that the "enemy" we are attacking is a decoy and that we are wasting time and energy in fighting the wrong battle. Take a moment and picture the person who is getting on your nerves right now. They are not your enemy. That coworker, your in-law, your spouse, that person writing negative comments on your social media account, they are not the enemy. As long as we are distracted from our purpose and fighting the decoy, we are exactly where the enemy wants us. Our battle is not against flesh and blood. 1 Peter 5:8 tells us our enemy is the devil. "Stay alert! Watch out for your great enemy, the devil. He prowls around like a roaring lion, looking for someone to devour"

(NLT). We are instructed to "Stand firm against him, and be strong in your faith" (1 Peter 5:9 NLT).

You might wonder, why are we talking about spiritual warfare in the middle of the spring season? Because it's important to understand that the natural and the spiritual worlds are connected. Just because spiritual warfare is not a popular topic does not mean it is not real. There's a famous line in the movie *The Usual Suspects* that says, "The greatest trick the devil ever pulled was convincing the world he didn't exist." And while that may be true for some, I think most people would say there is evil in the world. I think the greater trick has been in convincing the world that we are not in a spiritual battle. Because it can't be seen with our natural eyes, it does not seem to exist. However, a basic read of the New Testament will show that spiritual warfare is very real. I would just like to point out that the devil went after Jesus just before He stepped into His purpose in public ministry. If you are not familiar, "Jesus, full of the Holy Spirit, left the Jordan and was led by the Spirit into the wilderness, where for forty days he was tempted by the devil" (Luke 4:1–2 NIV). This was all before Jesus started His mission. My point is this: If the enemy was so bold to go after Jesus and prevent Him from walking in his purpose, how much more is he going to do the same to *us?*

Spring is a time of new beginnings, new life, open doors, new opportunities. Isaiah 43:18–19 puts it this way: "Forget the former things; do not dwell on the past. See, I am doing a new thing! Now it springs up; do you not perceive it? I am making a way in the wilderness and streams in the wasteland" (NIV). Having been on this spiritual journey for forty years, I can assure you that the enemy is not going to just stand by and let all these wonderful new things come into your life. No way! He is going to put up a fight to prevent what God is doing in your life. He is going to try and get you distracted, discouraged, deceived, depressed, or derailed from your purpose. There's a reason that tornadoes happen in the spring! Torna-does happen because cold and warm air patterns collide in spring. As you come out of your winter season and head toward summer, you need to anticipate some potential resistance in the spring. I say this not for us to walk around in fear, but to be aware and ready. So how do we prepare? Let's go back to what Paul wrote to the Ephesians:

> Finally, be strong in the Lord and in his mighty power. Put on the full armor of God, so that you can take your stand against the devil's schemes. For our struggle is not against flesh and blood, but against the rulers, against the authorities, against the powers of this dark world and against the spiritual forces of evil in the heavenly realms. Therefore put on the full armor of God, so that when the day of evil comes, you may be able to stand your ground, and after you have done everything, to stand. Stand firm then, with the belt of truth buckled around your waist, with the breastplate of righteousness in place, and with your feet fitted with the readiness that comes from the gospel of peace. In addition to all this, take up the shield of faith, with which you can extinguish all the flaming arrows of the evil one. Take the helmet of salvation and the sword of the Spirit, which is the word of God. And pray in the Spirit on all occasions with all kinds of prayers and requests. (Ephesians 6:10–18 NIV)

First, it's important to understand that our strength comes from the Lord, not from our talent, skills, power, or intellect. Second, just as the military puts on specific gear and uses weapons they have trained with for a physical battle, there are specific things we need for spiritual battles as well. We need to learn how to put on the specific gear Paul mentioned, from the belt of truth to the helmet of salvation. But I want to spend a moment on the two offensive weapons mentioned: the sword of the Spirit, aka the Word of God and prayer. In a spiritual battle, that is what we fight with. It is so important to pray and speak the Word of God over whatever situation you are facing. You do not come at that toxic person or issue in your workplace by cutting them with your words. You pray for them and speak the word of truth over the situation. There are entire books that have been written on this topic. I highly encourage you to take the time to learn more about the subject. Remember, the devil was once an angel and is well aware of spiritual things. Notice he went after Jesus in the wilderness using Scripture. We need to train in such a way that he does not know it better than we do!

The next time you get sideways with someone, or an issue is continuing to grow, remember that your fight is not against them. You are in a spiritual battle, and the devil wants to do whatever he can to keep you from walking in your purpose. He is definitely not happy about what the Lord has in store for you in the summer. When you find yourself in such situations, ask the Lord to open your eyes to see what He sees. Open your heart to the new thing He is doing. Ask him to continue the good work that He started in you. Give Him a blank sheet of paper and watch what He does. It is not a coincidence that paper is made from trees. Paper has been used for all types of amazing things from art masterpieces and classic works of literature and music, to toilet paper and money! But I think the most remarkable use is when we let Him write His purpose on our lives. As you do, He will take you on adventures, broaden your understanding, and transform you to be more like Him. You will essentially become "a letter from Christ" bringing love, hope, and peace to the world (see 2 Corinthians 3:3 NIV). That is how we truly flourish.

PART 4

SUMMER

unearthed from my journals:

3/30/11—my first home

Dear Lord, today I uttered words that I have been waiting to say for years: "I'm in escrow!" It's almost surreal. It's like when I someday will say "I'm engaged!" or "I'm pregnant!" or "I'm published!" Not only am I in escrow, but they want to close by April 25th! Thank you, Lord! I am so grateful!

7/11/17—the morning of the day I met my future husband but did not realize it

God—"the interview with the consultant is going to be significant"

7/21/17—after a 3-hour dinner with Phil following the evening session of the She Speaks conference

God—"He is your gift."

12/29/17

I'm engaged!!! Thank you, Jesus!!!

CHAPTER 10

An Interview to a Wedding

Summer brings long, hot days and short warm nights. The sun is shining brightly, birds are singing, and flowers are in full bloom. Plants and trees are adorned with lush green leaves and are producing fruit. Animals are breeding and at the peak of their activity. People head outside to play, travel, and bask in the sun. Everything around us is flourishing. Summer is a time of resting, relaxing, and being restored. It is also a time of celebration. Our prayers are answered, dreams have come to pass, and the season of waiting has come to an end. That is where I finally found myself after years of waiting.

"Grace, do you take Phil to be your lawfully wedded husband?" my pastor asked. I couldn't believe I was actually hearing these words. For so long, I had dreamed about this moment. Where it would take place, what I'd be wearing, and whose eyes I'd be looking into. And now, after years of waiting, it was finally here. I thought for sure the intimate gathering of family and friends could hear the beating of my heart through Pastor Jim's lapel mic. It was only eight months ago that

God whispered into my heavy heart: "The meeting with the consultant will be significant."

That was it. That's all I got during my prayer time the day I met Phil. He and his colleague were scheduled to interview the key staff members on our team. I had been an associate pastor on the team at my church for over fifteen years and was in charge of Leadership. Phil had come out of corporate America and started a ministry to help churches grow by focusing on systems, culture, structure, and organizational leadership. I did not know who my interview was with, or what it would entail, but after that heads-up from God, I made sure I was prepared. I had all the stats about my department ready. I had my *t*'s crossed and my *i*'s dotted. I was determined to have an answer for every question I was asked. Surprisingly, the conversation took a turn from what I'd expected. I wasn't asked many questions about my role or area of oversight. Instead, Phillip asked about my story and how I had started working at the church. He listened intently as I shared how my family had escaped the rule of Idi Amin in Uganda and fled to Duluth, Minnesota, in 1976. He was shocked to hear how the pastor of the first church we went to had asked our family to leave because the congregation was uncomfortable with a black family worshipping with them. He listened as I shared about the time our car tires were slashed and a brick was thrown through the living room window of our home simply because people did not want us in their neighborhood. He found it remarkable that, after such experiences, I had remained in church, not only as an active member of a congregation, but as a minister. Phillip was so captured by my story, he said I should write a book. I mentioned I had already written about my family story but didn't know how to get into traditional publishing. He recommended that I should attend the She Speaks conference, but added it was next week and he wasn't sure I could get in since there was a wait list. He offered to make a "Hail Mary" phone call, to which

I politely responded, "No, thank you." I had not heard of the conference, and I did not want to leave my job on such short notice without having things in place. Plus, I had just spent money earlier in the year attending two conferences and replacing a water heater.

However, when I got back to the office and talked to my coworkers, I discovered that my interview was really different than those of my colleagues, so I decided to google She Speaks. I was stunned to find out that it was for Christian writers and speakers and that part of the conference provided an opportunity to pitch your book idea to agents and publishers. I immediately knew I needed to be there. I went back to find Phillip after he'd finished his last interview and said that if there was any way for me to attend the conference, I would really like to go. He made a phone call, and long story short, I flew to North Carolina the following week for the conference. Turns out he was the chairman of the board for the organization that put on the conference.

As part of his role, Phillip also attended the conference with the other board members. He was one of the few men in a room of about eight hundred women. After I got situated in my hotel, I texted him to say thank you and to let him know I was looking forward to the conference. He suggested we meet fifteen minutes before the opening session and sit at the board table together. I was a little hesitant since he was my pastor's contact, but agreed to meet him there. When I got to the table, several of the board members greeted me by name. I wondered how they already knew who I was but dismissed it, because I was more concerned about the interview I had with one of the literary agents right after the morning session. In the whirlwind of completing a book proposal, a one-page bio sheet, and business cards in less than a week, I had not had a moment to think through what I was going to say to the agents. I was so nervous and really needed someone to pray for me. However, it was too early to call any of my friends on the West Coast, so I turned to Phillip and asked him to pray for me. He walked me to my interview, and we sat in a couple chairs outside the room. He held my hands and prayed a beautiful prayer. I cannot remember much of what he said because I was struck by how he was not intimidated by me being a pastor. I went to my interview and was surprised to find him waiting for me afterward, eager to hear how it went.

This is more than the regular amount of attention given when hosting a guest, I thought as I recounted the fifteen-minute interview. I brushed the thought away as I went to my breakout session, and he went to the board meeting. After the workshops, the conference attendees were on their own for dinner. Earlier in the day, I had learned that Phillip's birthday was the day before. He had not done anything to celebrate because he'd been on another business trip. As someone who celebrates birthdays for the entire month, I suggested we go do something for the special occasion. He made reservations at a nice Italian restaurant in the city and picked me up, looking very sharp in a white button-down shirt and black dress pants. He opened the car door for me as I got in wearing a burnt orange off-the-shoulder sheath dress.

Dinner was amazing. The ambiance was romantic, the food was delicious, and the conversation was engaging. Phillip was intelligent, compassionate, and attentive, and I could tell he was interested in me. However, I kept my distance. *Did I mention he was my lead pastor's contact…and he was fifteen years older than me?* As the dinner conversation continued, I found myself increasingly intrigued and wanting to know more about him. We ended up talking for three hours, after which he took me to see the city skyscape from the twenty-first floor of another building downtown. Afterward, he dropped me off at my hotel. We did not kiss, hug, or hold hands, but I could tell there was something sparking between us.

I went to my room and asked the Lord the same question I had asked each time a guy was interested in me: "Is this who You have for me?" Previously, each time, I had clearly heard "no." But that was not the case this time as I waited for an answer. "He is My gift to you," the Lord whispered in my heart. I sat down on the bed, stunned by what I'd just heard.

Was it really happening? Had I just spent the day and had dinner with my future husband? Was the man I had prayed for over two decades finally here? I did not sleep at all that night. I spent part of the time journaling and trying to capture the moment. The rest of the sleepless hours were spent googling couples that had more than a fifteen-year age gap and were still flourishing. All I came up with were CeCe Winans and her husband, Alvin Love II, and George and Amal Clooney.

The following morning, Phillip was leading a luncheon with the major donors for the ministry. As I sat in my breakout session, it suddenly dawned on me I could get the recording for the sessions and listen to them later. Instead, I should go and be present in what God was doing between Phillip and me. So I texted him and asked if he could meet me after he was done with the donor luncheon. I brought my journal and we sat down at an empty restaurant in the conference center. I told him I had a couple questions for him. I did not give him any context before diving into the first question. Please know I am not recommending a conversation like this after such a short acquaintance. I just needed to know if I had truly heard from God and that this was for real.

I opened my journal and started with my first question. "How do you feel about the age difference between us?" I asked with a straight face, looking him squarely in the eyes. Phil just about fell out of his chair. There was an awkward silence as he looked at me incredulously, trying to figure out where I was coming from. While he had clearly expressed an interest in me, I had not been as forthcoming. After collecting himself, he stammered, "I'm okay with it. How do you feel about it?" I told him I had spent the night googling couples in a thriving relationship where there was more than a fifteen-year age difference between them, and that there were only two couples I had discovered so far.

Next question, I muttered to myself. I was embarrassed by my own cluelessness. I should have realized that, from his perspective, it was awesome to be with a younger woman. I knew that Phil had two young adult daughters from his late wife. "How do you feel about children?" I asked. As if the first question was not direct enough, this one clearly went there. It seemed like an out-of-body experience to be having such a straight conversation, having just met Phillip a week prior. I had never asked a guy such a question. I was not desperate. I just needed to know if this really was from God. I had already settled in my heart when I turned forty that I was content whether or not I had kids. My heart's desire was to get married. After taking in the question and collecting his thoughts, Phillip respectfully said, "While it would be the greatest honor to have children with you, I feel like that stage in my life has passed." He looked surprised when I responded, "I'm okay with that."

Looking him straight in the eye, I said, "I have one more question." It was the only one I had asked other guys in the past. Their mediocre and subpar answers often determined that there would not be a second date. That being said, I was eager to hear how Phillip would respond. "What's your purpose in life?" I asked. When Phillip shared that his purpose was to build the Kingdom by building leaders in the church, I knew he was the one God had chosen for me. I have always believed that God brings two people together to do greater things for His Kingdom than they are doing on their own. I knew there were significant things He had called me to do, and most of the men who had previously expressed an interest in me did not mesh with that. When Phillip shared his vision, something sparked within me. I knew I could partner with and submit to that vision since it was essentially what was in my heart as well.

You might wonder where things went from there. How did we move forward after having such a straight conversation within a week of meeting each other? I knew what the Lord had put in my heart, but I did not share that with Phillip. I did not rush things or try to make things happen, but instead let them unfold in God's timing. Phil pursued me and began to court me. He flew out to Southern California several times and I went to visit him in Charlotte where I got to meet his daughters, who were home for the holidays. Although Phillip had dated a few other women, it had only been four years since they'd lost their mom to cancer, so I was not sure how they would receive me. While it was an adjustment, the girls were glad to see their dad happy and graciously welcomed me. Unbeknownst to me, before I arrived in Charlotte to be with everyone for Christmas, one of the girls had asked their dad if he felt I was the one. When he said yes, she asked him what he was waiting for. He told her that he wanted us all to have time together before taking the next step. The girls replied that they wanted to be part of the celebration while they were home for the holidays. So that day, the three of them went and picked out a ring and the girls helped Phillip come up with a plan to propose.

Later that week, Phillip picked me up from my Airbnb for a day trip to the Biltmore, a tourist attraction in the Blue Ridge Mountains of North Carolina. The historic 8,000-acre luxurious estate turned into a museum was built in 1889 and remains America's largest privately owned home. We parked and got on the shuttle to the mansion. As we got off the bus, Phillip said he wanted to take a picture on the bridge across the expansive lawn. I really wanted to head straight inside the building because the weather was so cold, but I agreed, because he rarely initiated taking selfies. We walked over to the bridge and found a spot to take a picture. "Could you take your sunglasses off?" he asked. I quickly removed them so we could hurry up and take the picture and get inside. "Could you take your gloves off?" he asked.

I looked to see if he was serious. It didn't make sense why I would need to take my gloves off for a picture. I had already mentioned to him how I did not like the cold—especially as an African woman born on the equator. However, Phillip had gone through so much trouble to plan the trip, I decided to go along with it. "Just be ready to take the picture really quick," I said as I pulled off my gloves and immediately put my hands in my jacket pockets. I wasn't excited about the picture because I was freezing and looked like a purple marshmallow with all the layers I had on. But we took the selfie with the Biltmore in the background, and then Phillip said he had something he wanted to say to me. Again, I looked at him to see why he was so intent on staying out in the cold and why on earth he couldn't say whatever he had to say inside, where it was warmer. As I was having this conversation in my head, I noticed he was lowering himself toward the ground. I thought, maybe he was just picking something up or setting something on the ground. I was too cold to catch any clue about what was happening.

Phillip still had his phone in his hand and began to read something from it. I wondered why he was trying to say something from down where he was—it seemed more effective to just speak into my ear. "Grace, I knew from the beginning that you were the one." I was so confused. Why couldn't he tell me that while we were inside the venue? Why did he have to kneel down…*OMG! Did he just get down on one knee? Is he about to ask me to marry him? Am I really in the middle of being proposed to? The moment I've dreamed about over so many years?!*

"You are my heart and I don't want to spend another day without knowing you will be my wife, growing together in Christ. Will you marry me and go on this adventure together?"

I stood frozen (figuratively and literally!), looking at the man on his knees in front of me. So many times, I had imagined what this moment would be like. And now it was really happening! Right here, right now, in front of all the strangers milling about and me looking like a purple marshmallow. I was so not prepared! *Stay in the moment, Grace*, I said to myself. Phillip's lips had stopped moving and he was looking up at me. After a few seconds of silence, I finally realized he was waiting for a response. I hadn't registered much of what he said after I realized I was in the middle of being proposed to. I just knew it was the time to say yes.

"Yes!" I said, barely able to move my lips or any other muscle in my body that had gone into shock.

My arms hung like two lead weights, frozen by my side. Phillip had to take my hand and draw it toward him to slip the ring on my finger (pictures from this moment showing how I clearly had no clue what was happening can be seen on my Instagram @gracewabuke-klein, or on my website). I gasped as I saw the diamonds glistening against my dark skin. It was more stunning than anything I could have imagined. Phillip stood up and I wrapped my arms, which were finally working, around him. I hugged him tight, partly in celebration of the moment and partly to confirm this was really happening and I wasn't just dreaming.

I heard people clapping and looked around to see a group of onlookers who had stopped what they were doing to watch and celebrate with us. I noticed there was a guy in the distance taking pictures of us with a telephoto lens camera. I thought it was a little odd and pointed him out to Phillip. He said the girls had come to be part of the celebration and had brought one of their friends who was a professional photographer to capture the moment. Once I had spotted them, they came and congratulated us. I tried hard to stay in the moment as we took more engagement photos around the grounds.

While they got coffee at the café, we called my parents. My mom immediately started crying and thanking Jesus. They were both overjoyed and so happy to finally see the answer to their prayers and my heart's desire. Afterward, Phillip and I continued our tour of the Biltmore. I really do not remember anything from the mansion—the ring on my finger blinded everything.

Once Phillip had proposed, the rest of my time in Charlotte involved discussing initial wedding plans. I wanted to get married before my forty-third birthday on March twenty-third, which gave me exactly two and a half months to put everything together—doable for anyone who has worked on a church staff! I had three of the most unique and special showers I had ever experienced. And for the sake of us all, there were no games! Our wedding overlooking the Pacific Ocean was more amazing than anything I had dreamed, planned, or imagined. There are pictures all over my social media and website celebrating the day my dream came true. Just as the Lord initially said, Phil is my greatest gift. We are loving life, walking in our purpose, and serving God together.

As a newlywed, I'm still celebrating this summer season. However, it comes after a very loooooong winter! As I said before, I believe God has a purpose for marriage, and that he brings two people together to do greater things for the Kingdom than they can do on their own. I was determined not to settle or compromise, but to wait for the one God had for me. I can honestly say that it is worth the wait! It's never easy, but it's always so much better to wait for God's best.

I share this story to encourage you, my friend. Whether you are in a fall, winter, or spring season, summer *is* coming. Just like the process of photosynthesis, things are happening now that you cannot see with your natural eye. Just as you cannot see wind, you see the effects of the wind; in the same way, you may not see what God is doing, but you will see the outcome. And when it does happen, when the Lord does finally answer your prayers, have a party to celebrate! Have the bridal shower, the baby shower, or the housewarming party. Participate in a cancer survivor event or throw one of your own! Have a celebration to renew your marriage vows, celebrate a friend's sobriety, or the return of a lost family member. Throughout the Bible we see that people were intentional in having banquets, parties, and celebrations for what the Lord had done.

During the summer months, nature is alive and not dormant. Breeding, feeding, and new life are taking place. There is lots of activity as animals mate and wind helps plants to scatter their seeds. Just as summer is a time to gather with friends and family for barbeques, road trips, vacations, and enjoying the outdoors, the summer season of life is also a time for fun and celebration.

Recently Phil and I hosted the gender reveal party for our first grandchild. It's a boy! We were still celebrating the joy of the exciting news when just four days later we found ourselves in the emergency room with my mom, who had suffered a medical emergency. Talk about living in the unknown and unexpected! I have found that it is possible to be in two seasons of life at the same time. To be celebrating something in the summer and walking through a very difficult situation in the winter. What do you do when you find yourself living in the intersection of the best of times and the worst of times? Where do you go when friends are no longer there for you? When people you thought were going to celebrate the fulfillment of your dream with you are jealous. And those you thought would always stand with you are the first to bail when a storm blows in. What do you do?

It reminds me of a young man who found himself in a similar situation when he had an incredible once-in-a-lifetime experience and, only seconds later, a near-death experience. Peter and Jesus' disciples were on a boat and struggling to maneuver it because of the strong waves. Since they were skilled fishermen, it should not have been a challenge for them to navigate their boat across a lake. They would have been accustomed to steering boats through all types of weather. But there was a purpose for this inclement storm. In the midst of the heavy winds, they saw Jesus walking on the water. Immediately Peter wanted not only to confirm that it was Jesus, but to be with Him. He realized it was better to be in a storm *with* Jesus than continue doing things his way *without* Him. Jesus called Peter to him, so Peter got out of the boat and stepped onto the water. He and the disciples must have been shocked when he did not immediately get submerged underwater. Instead, Peter took a step and then another. He began to walk on water as if he were walking on solid ground! It was something no one had previously done. I'd say he was having an awesome summer experience! That was until he looked around and saw the wind. Then he began to sink and cried out to Jesus to save him. Jesus reached out his hand and caught him.

When Jesus and Peter climbed into the boat, the wind died down and something shifted among everyone on the boat. They began to worship Jesus, proclaiming, "Truly you are the Son of God" (Matthew 14:33 NIV). Although they had listened to His teachings, heard His parables, and seen Him work miracles, for the first time, they finally understood who Jesus really was. Just as we discussed that the altar is a place of encountering God, the unexpected storm is also. The altar is an encounter that we intentionally decide to create as we choose to let go. On the other hand, the sudden storm in the middle of a summer season is unexpected and puts us in the position to react to whatever just erupted. It's in such moments that we need to make the intentional decision to turn to Jesus. As we flounder in the water, trying desperately not to drown, there is only so much our friends and family can do. Peter did not cry out to the other disciples in the boat. He recognized that the help he needed could only come from Jesus.

The wisdom we learn from this passage is that whether we are in a summer or a winter season, we need to look to Jesus. We want to look to Him and keep looking to Him whether we are in a storm or in a season of peace. Circumstances change, but He remains constant. We can look to Him for direction and guidance in the midst of the unknown and unexpected. He is not shaken by the turbulence of the storm because He knows He has authority over creation. He has power over the storm.

The next time you are enjoying the rays of the summer season and are suddenly struck by a storm, or if you find yourself currently in the midst of both, you can be encouraged that just as Jesus stretched out His hand to take hold of Peter, He will also stretch out His hand to take hold of you when you call on Him. He is not going to let you sink or fall. You just need to keep looking to Him and not focus on the waves crashing around you. Keep your eyes on the One who is able to calm the storm. Keep on looking to Him for all you need.

How do you look to Jesus? What do you say to Him and what do you do? It doesn't require much. Peter cried out only three words: "Lord, save me!" And Jesus saved him. In fact, the text says "*Immediately* Jesus reached out his hand and caught him" (Matthew 14:31 NIV, emphasis added). Jesus saw him, Jesus heard him, and Jesus caught him. I want to encourage you, in whatever you are facing today, Jesus sees you, Jesus hears your cry, and Jesus is able to catch you and keep you from falling. When you feel alone or not sure how you will go on, when you get the medical test results, when you see the actions of that family member, or when you just got laid off. We all fall in the water at some point in life. But we are not meant to stay there. After all, you don't drown by falling in the water. You drown by staying there. When you feel yourself sinking, you need to call on Jesus. Sometimes it takes a good friend to remind you or nudge you to do that. It's exactly what Phil did for me the other day.

The week my mom was in the hospital, I was so stressed, it started to affect my health. Phil kept telling me I needed to let go of the expectations I was putting on myself. I needed to give them to Jesus and go get some rest. When he saw that was not working, he did something that instantly got my attention. He took out a measuring tape and measured the width of my left shoulder. When I asked him what he was doing, he simply replied: "These shoulders are not big enough to carry the weight of the world that you are trying to put on them." I got the message loud and clear. I put down all the "bags" of worry, stress, frustration, and anxiety. I took off my "I've got to figure everything out" and my "planner" hats. I shut down my computer, turned off my phone, and forced myself to rest. Many times, that is the best thing you can do in a turbulent situation. I had to trust that God was in control and that, just as He did on the lake, He is able to calm the storm.

As I close this chapter, I want to encourage you to keep on looking to Jesus. He sees you and knows exactly where to find you. Keep on living your purpose. Keep on serving. Keep on walking by faith. The Lord is watching over you. Just as He did for Peter, He is able to rescue you in times of trouble. Keep growing deep roots through prayer, worship, and absorbing the Word of God. When the storm lifts, *and it will*, you will experience the joy and beauty of summer. I would love to hear all about it and share in that moment with you. We have been on a journey together, and I would love the honor of celebrating your answer to prayer, whether it be a spouse, the birth of a child, a new job, a healing, a financial breakthrough, or whatever miracle you are believing for. My hope is that when you enter your summer season, you will share your journey with others who are in a winter season and encourage them of the Lord's faithfulness. I'm excited for all that the Lord has in store for you in your summer season!

CHAPTER 11

If Rings Could Talk

Each year, trees form new cells in concentric circles known as annual growth rings. The alternating dark and light rings mark the years in the tree's life. The light-colored rings represent wood that grew in the spring and early summer, while the dark rings represent wood that grew in the late summer and fall. One light ring plus one dark ring equals one year of the tree's life. The rings also tell us information about the climate throughout the years. Because trees are sensitive to their surrounding conditions, the rings reveal events in the environment such as rain, fire, or drought that impacted how much the tree grew. In years of a drought, there is minimal growth. In warm and wet years, the tree rings are wider than in years when it is cold and dry.

When I learned this about tree rings, it made me start to wonder what the "rings" of our lives would reveal. Would they reveal growth, stagnation, scars from a fire, heartache from years of drought, or minimal growth from a painful wound? If the "rings" from my life could talk, what wisdom would they share? I may not have realized it at the time, but as I look back now and count the rings, I can see that

God was growing and transforming me. He was enabling me to flourish. The world equates flourishing with activity, productivity, expansion, and success. A Biblical perspective does not mean we *do more*; it means we *become more* like Christ.

The summer season of life provides a peaceful time to be able to process and reflect. Now that I'm in a summer season of my life, I want to leave you with some lessons I've learned along the journey.

There is greatness inside you

A seed may seem small and insignificant, but there is an entire tree hidden within it. It just needs the right resources such as soil, water, and sunlight to begin to develop. As the saying goes, every tree is simply a seed that did not give up.

Just like the seed, know that there is immense greatness within you. God put it in you and He wants to draw it out so you can flourish and walk in your purpose. We see Him doing that throughout the Bible and history. Abraham did not have any kids and became the father of nations; Joseph went from tending sheep to being thrown in prison to the governor in charge of the whole land of Egypt; Esther was an orphan who became queen and delivered her people from mass genocide; Gideon went from threshing wheat in a winepress to hide from the enemy to a fearless, mighty warrior who led his people to victory. Deborah became a judge giving counsel to the leaders of Israel; Mary became the mother of Jesus; Paul went from killing Christians to a passionate evangelist whom the Lord used to write much of the New Testament. Billy Graham, the son of a dairy farmer, became one of the greatest evangelists of all time and advisor to twelve US presidents, from Truman to Obama. The list goes on and on throughout history and continues today with you and me. Isaiah 61:3 says, "They will be called oaks of righteousness, a planting of the LORD for the display of his splendor" (NIV).

Growth is happening in the dark

Roots are mostly hidden, and we often cannot see them growing. But just because you cannot see the growth or change doesn't mean something isn't happening. It's the beautiful lesson that the bamboo tree teaches us. Let's say you planted a seed for a bamboo tree in the ground today. You diligently water and tend to it each day, making sure it has light and everything it needs for growth. After a month, there is no sign of anything growing, but you continue to water the ground. Three months go by, and you wonder if you have done something wrong in taking care of it. After a year with no sign of the shoot breaking through the ground, you are sure the seed did not germinate, and the tree is dead. However, you continue to water it because that's what the seed packet said to do. After another year of the same thing, you take the seed packet back to the store to see if perhaps the seed you planted might have been damaged and if you should get some new seed to start over. But they assure you that your plant is just fine and tell you to keep watering it. You go home and do as they say, but still there is no sign of growth. After a third year of watering the empty plot of dirt, your neighbors are starting to look at you funny, wondering why you are wasting your time. You are tempted to plant some flowers in the spot, but instead you start watering early in the morning before anyone is awake to question what you are doing. After a fourth year, you are done wasting your time. By this time, other things you planted have grown, but the bamboo tree still has no sign of life. Just as you are getting ready to dig up the ground and prepare it to grow something else, you remember the words of the person at the plant store: "Whatever you do, do not dig up the seed: just keep on watering the ground where you planted it." In frustration, you continue to water the ground for another year.

Then something unbelievable happens in the fifth year. A shoot breaks through the ground! It begins to grow rapidly, reaching four feet tall in twenty-four hours! In just over a month, it grows to ninety feet tall! Your neighbors come to see the tree that appears to have grown ninety feet in just five weeks. But you know the reality is that it grew ninety feet in five *years!* The strong, unseen root system that was developed over five years in the dark was what enabled the bamboo tree to grow tall and sustain life. Had you dug up the seed each year to see if it was growing, you would have stunted the tree's growth. Looking back over the years of frustration when you thought nothing was happening, you realize the tree was establishing a foundation to grow and fulfill its purpose. Had you stopped watering and fertilizing the tree, it would have died. Instead, all the years of being still, trusting in God's timing, and not trying to make something happen enabled it to flourish.

In life, some seasons last longer than others, and growth often happens without you seeing it. My winter season was two decades, and I would not wish that on anyone. The early years were not too hard, but as time went by and the number of available single guys grew slim, it became increasingly difficult. I was successful in every area of my life except for the one I really wanted.

For years I asked the Lord why He was having me wait so long. I never got an answer. Why did some people wait only two years to get married and I waited two decades? It was not until after I got married, that the Lord *finally* answered and simply asked, "Grace, would you rather have a faith that is two years deep or two decades deep?"

Immediately, I got it. The winter season had cultivated a level of faith and developed spiritual roots that no other season could have done. Although it was painful, the faith, wisdom, and spiritual maturity I developed over twenty years could not have happened in two years. *The winter seasons of life transform and empower you in ways that cannot happen in the fall, spring, or summer.*

My friend, although the winter months—the unknown and unexpected seasons—are challenging, there are things that can be learned and developed only as you walk through them. I encourage you to embrace the insights the Lord is revealing to you, the character development taking place, and to reflect on how you are growing and being transformed through your journey. Hopefully you, too, will be able to inspire others along their journey someday.

I encourage you to be open to the possibility that even though you may not be getting the answer you are praying for, that doesn't mean He's not answering other things. Just like we cannot see the daily changes in a tree's growth with our natural eye, you may not realize the changes that are taking place in your life. But as you look back over the years and decades, you will see strong roots, growth rings, and transformation.

God is in the waiting

In our culture, we do not like to wait. We have grown accustomed to instant transportation, instant food, instant purchases, and instant information. However, God is not on our timetable. He often leverages seasons of waiting for His glory and for our spiritual growth. Psalm 37:7 tells us, "Be still in the presence of the LORD and wait patiently for him to act" (NLT). God has not forgotten you in the silence. In the waiting, He is calling you to Him. That same longing in your heart is how He longs to be with you. To teach you things and show you things that you would not see if you had your blessing. Just as trees do not strive to make something happen, we also want to wait patiently and just be. From trees, we can be assured that everything in life happens at the right time. We can trust God's timing.

If the growth rings could talk, I believe they would say that God is in the waiting. It's through this process that He draws us close and teaches us how to pray. A young tree whimpers, "When, God, *when?*" or "Why *me*, God?" or "It's not *fair*, God!" or "How *come*, God?" but a more mature tree whispers, "It does not make sense, but I trust You, God…Lord, it's not happening in my timing, but I trust You and Your timing…You are good, You are faithful, and my life is in Your hands." A seasoned tree has established deep roots in the Lord's presence and developed an assuredness that He does answer our prayers. The answers may not look like what we anticipated or come in the time we prefer, but God is faithful. Through the process, there has been a shift in our focus. The focus is on being with Jesus, and expressing love, praise, and thanksgiving to Him. Our desire is getting to know Him more and becoming more like Him. The thing we are believing for is no longer a source of frustration, worry, or heartache. It has been placed in the Lord's hands. The mature tree confidently waits for what is already done in the spiritual, to manifest in the natural. As they expectantly trust God, their prayers have turned to thanksgiving for what He has already done. "This is the confidence we have in approaching God: that if we ask anything according to His will, He hears us. And if we know that He hears us—whatever we ask—we know that we have what we asked of Him" (1 John 5:14–15 NIV).

Another thing I've noticed about mature trees is that they do not get bent out of shape when another tree is planted beside them and starts to grow at a faster pace. They don't get jealous or sick with envy when the other tree starts producing leaves, flowers, or fruit before them. The mature tree just continues to focus on what it can control, namely itself.

Relationships are vital for life

I was watching a TED talk about trees the other day. The forest ecologist said that forests have an underground world of "infinite biological pathways that connect trees and allow them to communicate and allow them to behave as though it's a single organism."[*] In other words, trees talk to each other! There is a massive communications network below the ground. Who *knew*? What are they talking about, you ask? Essentially resources and best practices for healthy growth. Trees help one another adapt to their environment by sharing information and nutrients to help them grow strong and healthy. They are linked together by fungi called mycelium that travel back and forth and increase the resilience of the whole community. When one tree gets sick, the other trees help it get better by sending it special sugars through its roots.

Just like trees, we need relationships. God created us to be in community. Hebrews 10:24–25 encourages us, "And let us consider how we may spur one another on toward love and good deeds, not giving up meeting together, as some are in the habit of doing, but encouraging one another—and all the more as you see the Day approaching" (NIV). In his letter to the Philippians, Paul encourages them to imitate the humility of Christ:

> Do nothing out of selfish ambition or vain conceit. Rather, in humility value others above yourselves, not looking to your own interests but each of you to the interests of the others. In your relationships with one another, have the same mindset as Christ Jesus: Who, being in very nature God, did not consider equality with God something to be used to his own advantage; rather, he made himself nothing by taking the very nature of a servant, being made in human likeness. And being

---

* Suzanne Simard, "How Trees Talk to Each Other." TEDSummit, June 2016, https://www.ted.com/talks/suzanne_simard_how_trees_talk_to_each_other/transcript.

found in appearance as a man, he humbled himself by becoming obedient to death—even death on a cross! (Philippians 2:3–8 NIV)

Neither one of these passages can be applied in our lives unless we are in community with others. That is how we support one another and make each other stronger. Yes, relationships can be messy, but they cause us to grow in our character. Probably the most well-known verse when it comes to community is found in Proverbs 27:17: "As iron sharpens iron, so one person sharpens another" (NIV). We can see this in nature, too. Mature trees help smaller trees in their vicinity by transferring water, carbon, and other resources through the underground fungal networks. Without such cooperation, the new generation of trees would not be able to survive. What a great example in showing us the importance of having mentors in our lives and being a mentor to others.

Be your authentic, unique self

No two trees are the same. Each one grows without copying another tree. Can you imagine if all trees were the same or if they were all trying to be like one "influencer" tree? There would not be the majestic giant sequoias, the breathtaking southern live oaks, or the playful palm trees. There would not be the magical changing color of leaves in the fall or the cherry blossoms that bloom in the spring. How boring and drab the world would be! Thankfully trees fully embrace who they are and are content in being themselves. No tree is stressed out that another tree has grown or "achieved" more than it has in a certain span of time. Each tree species gracefully accepts its characteristics, qualities, and development. Like trees, we each, in our uniqueness, add beauty to the world. We have each been created with gifts, talents, and abilities to share with others. You will not be able to fulfill the purpose you put on this earth for if you are consumed with trying to be like someone else. This applies to you, your business, your ministry, and your career. You have your purpose and they have theirs.

This is so easy for some people to do, but for some of us, it can be very challenging. I know because as a young girl I mastered the art of being a chameleon and becoming like whatever environment I was in. Because I was so often teased for being different in my predominantly white and Asian schools, I learned how to quickly read a room and assimilate. My experience was that being myself resulted in people making jokes about me, so I focused on learning everything about their culture in an effort to fit in. Instead of bringing all of me into the room and adding to the conversation or elevating the environment, I left all that at the door…for years. How did I overcome that and finally embrace just being myself? A lot of the transformation happened through what we discussed earlier in Chapter 2. I discovered my identity as I read the Bible and embraced what God said about me. As you read the Word of God, you will discover not only your identity in Christ, but also your purpose and the authority He has given you. Just as God created each snowflake and each tree different from all the rest, He has also uniquely created you. You were born an original, so don't die a copy.

Embrace God's timing for change

Just as the natural seasons change, so do the seasons in our lives. Ecclesiastes 3:1 tells us, "For everything there is a season, and a time for every purpose under heaven" (web). While you may not like your current circumstance or season, know that it has a purpose. God is doing something that you cannot see or understand from your perspective. Ecclesiastes 3:11 assures us, "[God] has made everything beautiful in its time" (niv). We should not judge our life based on only the current season in our life. It is part of God's bigger plan and purpose for our lives. We need to get comfortable with embracing His timing. We need to trust that although it may not look like it now, things will change. We do that by following the leading of the Holy Spirit instead of holding on to our timeline of when or how things are supposed to happen. Trees do not try to bypass, rush, or fight the seasons, but instead they embrace God's timing for change. We also would be wise to do likewise. I like this quote, attributed to Bruce Lee: "Notice that the stiffest tree is most easily cracked, while the bamboo or willow survives by bending with the wind." The bamboo tree teaches us the value of being flexible with timing and accepting of change.

But what about when your current circumstances do not line up with what you know to be true about God? That's when you have got to trust that He is God and that He is madly in love with you. There is so much more to Him that we have yet to learn. One of the ways I do that is by cultivating a sense of wonder. I grew up in church, I've read through the Bible, I know the stories and principles, I went to seminary and have taught classes on the Bible and how to study it—but I know there will always be more to learn about the Word of God and who He is. My desire is to keep learning and growing in my knowledge of Him. One of the specific ways I do that is by watching the Nature Channel. I know it's not what is trending on Netflix, but there is something so powerful about seeing God's creation. As I learn about different species whether underwater, on land, or in the air, I am in awe of God and all He created. As I see the specific details for each species and the unique abilities He created in them to survive, my sense of wonder grows. It gives me assurance that He is aware of all the details in my life. I can trust that even though things may be changing, or the circumstances are not what I would prefer, He's got me.

That's what trees teach us. Imagine being a young tree experiencing the fall season for the first time. You would probably freak out. The beautiful leaves you started growing in the spring became a lush green crown in the summer and transformed into stunning shades of red, orange, yellow, and brown. And just as you were enjoying the delightful creation you had evolved into, something inside you begins initiating all your exquisite leaves to be released. In a panic, you try to hang on to the leaves and collect the ones the wind has carried to the ground. You are alarmed that you are losing a major part of who you are. Something of great value that you worked hard to create. You feel naked, bare, and begin to lose hope as you seemingly regress. But then you notice the older trees around you are also losing their leaves and they do not look concerned. They have a perspective that you don't: Spring will come once again. Leaves will bud and grow once again.

That's essentially what the rings of a tree tell us: Seasons change. It might be winter in your life right now, but my friend, summer will come. Keep believing and do not lose faith that you will see that answer to prayer. That you will walk down the aisle. You will hold your baby in your arms. You will be healed. That relationship will be restored. You will experience joy and laughter again. The thing we need to understand in the process is that spiritual seasons are on a different timetable than the natural ones. Some spiritual seasons last for months, some for years, and others for decades. We need to be open to God's timing and how He chooses to answer our prayers. They may not always look like we anticipated, but we soon find out it's what's best for us. Isaiah 55:8–9 says, "'For my thoughts are not your thoughts, neither are your ways my ways,' declares the Lord. 'As the heavens are higher than the earth, so are my ways higher than your ways and my thoughts than your thoughts'" (NIV). In what you are facing today, I encourage you to ask God for His perspective and to be open to what He is doing in His timing, especially when it does not seem to make sense. Just as it does not make sense for a tree to intentionally release its leaves, there is always a reason, always something that we will receive from the Lord as we trust Him.

Do the necessary work for healing

Trees sometimes get injured by accidents or attacked by diseases, creating orange spots on leaf surfaces, causing their texture to be littered with holes or to look like the branches have been scorched by fire. Fortunately, trees have the ability to heal themselves. To address diseases, trees remove the infected leaves and branches so the disease does not spread. In the case of injuries, tree cells change course and flow around the wound, creating a knot. This enables the cells within the wood grain to continue supplying nutrients and water to other parts of the tree.

When we face adversity, we also need to do the necessary work for healing so we can continue to grow.

Many of us experience emotional injuries more than physical ones. Often the healing process for them takes a lot more time and effort. But if we want to walk in our purpose and flourish, we need to do the necessary work for healing. In other words, we don't ever want to let our hearts get to a permanent place of hurt or offense where we are closed off to what God wants to do in and through us. I know it can be so hard at times. I admit there have been many times when I blew it. People can be so hostile. What I've found to be helpful is to have a good cry, let it all out, and then do what Jesus did. Get back on mission. That's exactly what He did when He almost got canceled as He started His public ministry. When the mob, angered by what He said, was ready to throw Him off a cliff, Jesus "walked right through the crowd and went on his way" (Luke 4:30 NIV). In the passages immediately following the near-death attack, we find

Jesus teaching and healing people in another town. In other words, He stayed on mission. He kept on loving people, healing people, and teaching them about the Kingdom of God. That is my prayer for you and me.

Throughout the Bible, we see people who experienced personal attacks and struggles. What we read time and time again is how in the midst of whatever they were going through, they chose to magnify the goodness and faithfulness of God. You see, we all have a choice as to what we choose to magnify. Replaying what was said or done to you is magnifying the other person's voice over God's voice in your life. That is not His desire for our lives. He wants us to see things from His perspective. Two people who did that so well and always inspire me whenever my perspective is off are Joseph from the Old Testament and Paul from the New Testament. If you recall, Joseph was sold by his brothers into slavery, wrongfully accused of assault, and thrown into prison. Twenty-two years later when he revealed to his brothers who he was as the one in charge of the whole land of Egypt, there was a *lot* he could have said or done to his siblings. There's a lot I would have said and done to them on his behalf! But Joseph had learned to see things from God's perspective. He told them, "It was to save lives that God sent me ahead of you....God sent me ahead of you to preserve for you a remnant on earth and to save your lives by a great deliverance....it was not you who sent me here, but God. He made me father to Pharaoh, lord of his entire household and ruler of all Egypt" (Genesis 45:5, 7–8 NIV). After their father died and the brothers were concerned that Joseph would now pay them back for their wrongs, Joseph told them, "You intended to harm me, but God intended it for good to accomplish what is now being done, the saving of many lives" (Genesis 50:20 NIV).

Paul also had the same perspective while writing from a prison cell in chains. He said, "What has happened to me has actually served to advance the gospel" (Philippians 1:12 NIV). Both responses absolutely blow my mind. One of them referred to the wrongs people had done to him and the other to the situation he was in. They did not retaliate, complain, attack, or seek vengeance. They both realized that God uses people and circumstances to draw us closer to Him and fulfill His purpose. Both Joseph and Paul saw their unknown, unexpected, and unwanted situations from His perspective. That is what God wants to reveal to us as well. I pray that you and I will seek and embrace the Lord's perspective in our situations.

Set healthy boundaries

Have you ever noticed that the branches of the tree do not try and carry the entire weight of the tree? They leave that up to the trunk of the tree. In the same way, we need to know that the whole world does not rest on our shoulders. Setting boundaries is vital for healthy growth. It can be so hard to do and sometimes even counterintuitive. Take, for example, when you're on a plane and the flight attendant is going over emergency procedures. One of the things they always say is that in the case of loss in cabin pressure, oxygen masks will fall from the ceiling. Then they always emphasize that if you are traveling with a child or someone who needs help, you are to put the oxygen mask on yourself first. Most of us would naturally go to put it on the child first. But the reason behind the specific order is that we have got to make sure we are safe (and healthy) in order to help others. A tree that refuses water and sunlight for itself can't bear fruit for others. It's normal to want to help people we love. And a lot of the time it is a good thing. However, when a friend or a family member is playing Russian roulette with their physical, mental, or emotional health, you cannot be the emergency response system. It will begin to severely impact your health. You will not be able to remain healthy if you are fighting for their health more than they are for themselves. Some of us feel horrible when we need to set boundaries with someone we care about. There are so many resources available to help with that and I encourage you to utilize them.

Let go to live

The growth rings of any deciduous tree would say that you have got to let go in order to live. We need to let go of our negative thoughts, bad habits, offenses, and limiting beliefs. All of these drain our energy and prevent us from walking in our purpose. Earlier we talked about how if trees do not shed their leaves, they will eventually die. That was because when temperatures drop very low, the water in the leaves would freeze. Another reason that trees shed their leaves is to lose the extra weight before the snow comes. Branches with extra weight from leaves and snow would break much easier. And by shedding their leaves, trees are able to withstand harsh storms because the strong winds have nothing to grasp on to and bring the tree down. Without any leaves, the wind just blows through the trees. Likewise, when we hang on to negative things, we are more likely to break under the mounting weight.

We experience freedom when we let go of things. I recently tried working out on a treadmill wearing wrist and ankle weights. Each weighed five pounds, for a total of twenty pounds. It may not seem like much, but you will definitely notice it while power walking on an incline. Because my body was already feeling sluggish as I started working out early in the morning, I put the weights on for the first fifteen minutes and then stopped briefly to take them off. Something amazing happened when I got back on the treadmill. I felt so much lighter. With the weights off, I increased my speed and walked faster and farther. I felt like an Olympic athlete for the remaining forty-five minutes. The rest of the workout was so much easier and seemed to go by quickly. Who has ever said a workout went by fast! But that's exactly what I experienced when I removed the weights.

In life, there are weights we have taken on that are slowing us down and preventing us from living our lives to the fullest. Perhaps you took on responsibility for things that were never yours to carry. It may be a situation that has you worried and staying up all night, a relationship that is causing you stress, your finances, your health, the state of things in the world right now, the things that are unknown and up in the air, the list is endless. And if each thing represents a five-pound weight, pretty soon we are trying to walk through life carrying an extra thirty, forty, or fifty pounds. Not only will you barely be able to move, but you definitely will not be living your life to the fullest. You will be so much more effective and productive when you put the weights down and no longer let them burden your heart and mind. I encourage you to give the issues to Jesus. Psalm 55:22 instructs us to "Cast your cares on the Lord and he will sustain you; he will never let the righteous be shaken" (NIV). Take comfort in knowing that He will carry you through whatever you are facing.

If the growth rings on any mature tree could talk, I believe they would all encourage us to live life to the fullest. To let go of the things that are holding us back, not to sweat the small stuff, not to put things on hold until the perfect timing, not to carry burdens we were never meant to bear but rather live our life. They would tell you that storms will come, but with time, they will pass. They would tell you not to be concerned about that tree that is being planted close to you—there is plenty of sun, water, and soil for everyone. Keep on living your life. They would tell you to embrace new opportunities and continue to grow. They would remind you that *it is the thief that comes to steal, kill, and destroy. Jesus came that you may have life and have it to the full* (see John 10:10 NIV). Do your growth rings show a life that is lived to the full? One that is walking in the purpose God has for it? When we look back at our "growth rings," we don't want to see one consecutive hold-ing pattern. "I'll do that, when this happens." I'll buy a home when I get married. I'll start the business once the kids are grown. I'll go back to school when I retire. I want to encourage you to live your life now and stop waiting for the "perfect" time, because there will always be a time that seems better than now. So go on that adventure, travel the world, run a marathon, take a class, learn to play an instrument, serve in your church, give back to your community, mentor kids, become an investor. Let's not let anything hold us back from flourishing and living life to the fullest.

Rest

It has become normal in our society to be constantly busy. Whether it be from work, kids, activities, social events, or social media, our schedules are packed. We have FOMO (fear of missing out) at the thought of not being part of things, and so we keep going and going. However, being constantly busy is not how God designed for us to live. He wants us to work and rest. He himself rested after creat-ing the world. Throughout the Bible there are stories and principles emphasizing the importance of times of rest. Probably the most well known is the Sabbath. The word means "cease from labor." The Lord first introduced it to the Israelites as part of the Ten Command-ments. "Remember the Sabbath day by keeping it holy. Six days you shall labor and do all your work, but on the seventh day is a sabbath to the LORD your God. On it you shall not do any work....For in six days the LORD made the heavens and the earth, the sea, and all that is in them, but he rested on the seventh day. Therefore the LORD blessed the Sabbath day and made it holy" (Exodus 20:8–11 NIV). I'd say the fact that God included it in the Ten Commandments makes it pretty important! In fact, in the Old Testament, those who did not observe the Sabbath were to be put to death. Thankfully, that is no longer the case, but we can see how the Sabbath was not only holy, it was a covenant.

In the New Testament, Hebrews 4:9–10 says, "There remains, then, a Sabbath-rest for the people of God; for anyone who enters God's rest also rests from their works, just as God did from his" (NIV). God wired rest into nature. Many animals go into hibernation in the winter. Trees go dormant and minimize their metabolic activity to conserve energy. On a daily basis we rest by going to sleep at night. There have been numerous studies showing the value of specific hours of sleep. However, what is not as readily talked about is having a weekly day of rest. That could involve spending time in solitude, being still, reflecting, enjoying time just talking and eating with friends. If taking a whole day is not possible with your life stage of raising kids, try maybe taking a half day or starting with an hour.

Taking time to be still and reflective provides peace, rejuvenation, and valuable insights to help you grow. If the growth rings of a tree could speak, I believe they would encourage you to rest and be still. To be completely present and not lost in your thoughts and concerns about the past or the future.

Leave a legacy

We have been created to produce meaningful fruit. What good would an avocado tree be if it never produced any avocados? For a Christian, this is the fruit of the Spirit: love, joy, peace, patience, kindness, goodness, faithfulness, gentleness, and self-control (see Galatians 5:22 NLT). For so many years, I was so focused on my plans—when and how is my husband coming?—that I almost missed God's plan. I was so busy making my agenda and my lists that I almost missed the Divine purpose that God was asking me to be present for. God's plan involved a Man (Jesus) who had already come and was waiting for me to be with Him. To join *His* adventure. You see, God is always doing more than just answering our prayers. His plan involves us drawing close to Him and being in His presence. Learning what pleases Him, what breaks His heart, what His desire is. His plan involves us discovering our identity in Him, our value, our worth, our purpose, and the authority He has given us. My plan revolved around figuring out where I needed to be and what I needed to do for my husband to find me. Nothing wrong with that. There was just more to the story. God's story. God's plan involves His bride, the Church, preparing for His return. I realized God was trying to show me something I wasn't praying for. God, in His goodness, wasn't ignoring me. In whatever you are facing today, know that God sees you and He hears the cry of your heart. He has not forgotten you, and He is not ignoring you. As you look back at your growth rings, I believe you will see that the Lord is growing you through the unknown and unexpected seasons of your life. He is drawing you close to Him, transforming you to become more like Him, and inviting you to be part of His adventure and leave a legacy of love, hope, and peace in this world.

Yesterday I went on a long walk along a trail in our neighborhood. The crisp November air felt refreshing after the long week. Other than an occasional squirrel scurrying through the trees, the only sound was of my feet crunching the leaves on the ground. It is my favorite time of year to be outside and enjoy the beauty of the red, orange, and yellow leaves falling from the trees. As I looked at the carpet of colored leaves on the ground, it suddenly struck me that, only months ago, they had been part of the green canopy adorning the trees. What was once about twenty to forty feet in the air attached to the crown of a tree was now on the ground being trampled on. What was once part of a grand living organism was now by itself, unattached, and lifeless on the ground. And yet the leaves were not alone. They were joined with hundreds and thousands of other leaves. And not just from the same tree, from all different types of trees. Together they were about to undergo one of nature's beautiful cycles. Earthworms, microbes, and invertebrates in the soil shred plant material into small pieces. Then fungi, bacteria, and mold continue the process of decomposition. The broken-down leaves make nutrients available for trees to sustain their future growth.

Unlike trees, which live for decades or even centuries, most leaves are born in the spring, live throughout the summer, and die in the fall. Thankfully we live longer than leaves, but what struck me about their life cycle is that no matter what season they are in, they are living out their purpose. Whether in life or in death, leaves have a purpose in nature's ecosystem. At the peak of their life, they are serving as a food-generating machine for the tree they are attached to. They do not get upset or offended when the tree releases them. Instead, they recognize that there is a purpose for that release, too. As they fall from such a place of grandeur, only to be tossed about and trampled on, the leaves don't get up and try to attach themselves to another tree. They understand that particular season has passed, and they are now in a new one. They embrace each part of their life cycle because they know each one has a purpose. We also can live our lives with purpose whether we are in a position of power, fame, and influence or if we are in a season of obscurity, unnoticed and overlooked. Whether we are in our youth or the later stages of life, we can make an impact in the world around us. When we walk in our purpose, we are setting up the next generation to go further and achieve more.

One of the ways I have been able to look back on the "growth rings" of my life is through my journals. For over twenty-five years I have written my thoughts, prayers, and cries of my heart. I've also written the words and promises the Lord has given me. What He has taught me, the prayers He answered, and what I'm learning through the Word. I start a new journal almost every year. I put color-coded tabs on pages where there is something significant I need to remember. Red is for things I need to stop saying or doing. Green is for things I need to start or grow in. Yellow is for promises and truths in His Word. Pink is for answers to prayer. If I'm out of a particular color, any of the others work; the point is to just be able to note the page so I can go back to it later. At the end of each year, I take some time to reflect and read through all the Lord did throughout the year. Something really important that I do on the last page of the journal is to write down the key dates and events from the year. That makes it easy to look back at each year at a glance. Doing that for several decades has helped me clearly see the growth rings in my life. It has increased my faith and trust in God as I've seen His faithfulness over the years. If you have not journaled before, I highly encourage you to add this practice to your faith journey. I've created a resource to help you get started. You can go to gratitudewithgrace.com to get your journal, some additional resources, and get started today.

Well, my friend, I can't believe we are already at the end of this part of our journey. It has been a delight to walk through it with you. Thank you for allowing me to share my story and what God has done in my life. I would love to hear your story of what the Lord has been teaching you, and how I can be praying for you. You can message me on gratitudewithgrace.com. It would be the greatest joy to celebrate with you when your summer season comes. I am praying for you and cheering you on! *"May the Lord cause you to flourish"* (Psalm 115:14 NIV).

Hidden in Plain Sight

The Story from Phil's Perspective

The day I met Grace was both unexpected and significant. It was one of those God moments that changes the trajectory of your life. I was just coming out of an extended winter season, losing my wife to cancer and raising my two daughters. I had lost my partner, but not my purpose. I was once again focused on developing leaders and helping churches grow. I am deeply grateful for my winter season of loss and struggle. It gave me an incredible sense of value for every moment and every relationship. Practicing gratitude kept me going through that winter season. I learned that no matter what we lose, God is never a debtor. He always brings blessings that exceed the burden. It may not be in the form or timing we are praying for, but eventually He brings blessings greater than what we are capable of asking for or imagining.

God has never wavered from His promises, but it seemed in my spring season He was focused on blessing me in the vocational area of my life. I had started up focus412, an organizational leadership coaching and consulting ministry to help churches grow. I was flourishing in my purpose and loving being able to make a difference, but didn't have someone to partner and share it with. With how God had grown my heart for Him and His people (the church), I knew deep down inside that if I ever found someone, she would have to be incredibly deep in her relationship with Christ and love His church. What I do requires that. I run to the hard stuff, because the struggle is where significance is found.

Your purpose always has an element of pain. My pain is travel, but in order to develop leaders, you have to be in a relationship with them, which requires proximity. So about 150 days a year I am away from home, traveling to every corner of the United States. On this particular trip, I was in Southern California, about as far from my home in Charlotte, North Carolina, as you can get. It was a new church relationship and engagement. I was unusually tired, coming off several back-to-back trips and a three-hour time zone change. I am disciplined in my personal health so I knew I was running on empty and needed to be refreshed. I shared that with Philip, my incredible friend and coaching partner, as we prepared for the first day of our engagement with the church leadership team. Flipping through the staff interview bios, lining up our day, I had a strange sense I was supposed to talk with Grace Wabuke. What I sensed in my spirit was that my time with her would be refreshing. Little did I know my life was about to change.

So later that morning, after I'd completed a few interviews with team members, it was time for the Grace Wabuke interview. The first few interviews had been in an incredibly chilly office space, so when Grace walked in, I asked if she would mind if we found a warmer space so I could thaw out. She responded "yes!" and immediately moved toward the door. As we walked to the outdoor courtyard, I couldn't help but become more curious about her. She had such an incredibly joy-filled spirit. Why was it so evident? Where did it come from? It was mesmerizing.

We sat down across from each other in the sun. I thanked her for coming and started by asking her to tell her story. It's a way of quickly developing context and engagement. Grace began to share her story. She was describing some of the most difficult things anyone could experience, but never broke from her deeply joyful and grateful state. When she got to one of the many "what did she just say???" moments and said that her family had been asked to leave their church by their pastor because of the color of their skin, I was marked in that moment. My mind could not reconcile what I just heard: *You were kicked out of a church as a little girl because of the color of your skin and you chose after that to go to seminary and give your life to pastoring in the local church?* Once I'd collected myself, I remember thinking how she must really "get" who God is and understand what He intended for His church. I thought she must understand the difference between the church and people doing bad things in the church. It told me how deep her gratitude and forgiveness must be. I was experiencing someone who had faced incredible pain, but never blamed, compromised, or wavered in her faith. This was someone who had doubled down on God's promises and had lived out her purpose, despite the pain. That level of faith and purpose is what made her so fascinating and compelling. It was pure. It was earned. It was embedded. It was ready for whatever came next.

Grace's inner and outer beauty made it difficult to think about anything other than how unique, rare, and valuable she was. But how could she be single? It was as if she had been hiding in plain sight. Grace's unknown and unexpected seasons of life had formed in her the very strength, substance, and purpose that attracted me to her. The very things that caused her such incredible pain, God used to form the presence I was experiencing. I only knew what I saw back then, but after being in her life over the past five years, I now more fully understand how God shaped and formed her in the fire. Being different, not settling, leading and developing leaders, and investing in others in her time of greatest personal need. The list goes on but I would be remiss for not mentioning a personal favorite of mine, her physical features. Yes, those very features she was teased about are the most beautiful and wondrous things to me. Her incredible lips, her eyes, her hair. They are deep and mesmerizing. They are like priceless jewelry worn with humility and gratitude by a daughter of the King.

Grace always says that God brings two people together to do greater things than they would have done on their own. I have experienced that over and over again since Grace and I became one. Once I asked her to marry me, it felt like a seismic shift. As if someone had unlocked the vault to the rest of what God had been storing up for both of us. It opened up a bigger world and a greater understanding.

Our pain and purpose have been joined together to do greater things. Our purposes have become more powerful together than they ever could have been apart. In a unique and magical way, we both know that none of it is about us or our union. It's all about God's grace and mercy. His loving promise of eternal life. After all, He is the author and creator of all things. He knew how this all played out before it ever started.

ACKNOWLEDGMENTS

There are some assignments we receive from God that seem so big and impossible, you know there is no way you can complete them on your own. Assignments so outside of your strengths and comfort zone that you are convinced the Lord should have given them to someone else. This was one of those assignments. The fact that the Lord asked me, whose last English class was in high school, is still confounding to me. So when I say this book could not have been written without the tribe that the Lord assembled, it is for real. I am forever grateful to the people who came alongside me to write this book and live the stories in it.

Phil, you are my greatest gift from God. You have shown me how the winter season was more than worth the wait. Thank you for seeing with spiritual eyes what was hidden in plain sight. You have shown me God's love and grace in ways I never knew. Thank you for walking with me through every step of this writing journey. Your belief in me and the message God put in my heart continues to breathe oxygen to my soul. Thank you for being my number one encourager through every step of this process. You always knew the words to speak life when I was overwhelmed, discouraged, or stressed. Thank you for lovingly providing the space for me to write and your patience through the journey. I love you!

Thank you, Dad and Mom, for introducing me to the Lord at

a young age and teaching me how to grow in my walk with Him. I would not be who I am today without you. Thank you for the Godly legacy you passed down to me. Thank you to my family for your love, support, and prayers.

Thank you, Dr. Jim and Marguerite Reeve, for speaking into my life and raising me up in ministry. You saw something in the young college student still trying to figure out the call of God. Thank you for embracing me as a spiritual daughter and teaching me how to serve Him wholeheartedly.

Thank you, Pastor Chris and Tammy Hodges, for your leadership and friendship. Whenever people ask me how this California girl landed in the deep south, I love telling them about Church of the Highlands. As I write this, we are currently gathering as a church in numerous locations every morning for twenty-one days of fasting and prayer. It is my favorite thing we do as a church and what drew Phil and I to Birmingham, Alabama. Thank you for cultivating a culture and environment for us to seek the heart of God.

Thank you, Bob Goff, for believing in me and cheering me on from the moment we met. You called out dreams in me and spoke life to them. I have never had a conversation with you where I didn't leave encouraged and inspired. You continue to teach me how to love, and to be available and fully present with people. You inspire me to see and champion the one.

Thank you, Pastor Dino and DeLynn Rizzo, and Pastor Layne and Rachel Schranz, for the roles that you have played in the lives of Phil and I. We are forever grateful for how the Lord used you to have Phil and my paths cross. You have been amazing friends and encouragers in our lives and throughout this book writing process.

Thank you, Bill Jensen, for seeing something in me during our initial conversation at the She Speaks conference and for inviting me to be part of the William K Jensen Literary Agency. Thank you, Teresa

Evenson, for coming alongside me as my agent and very graciously guiding this first-time author through the book writing, editing, and publishing process. I am forever grateful for the wisdom, insight, perspective, and support you provided. Thank you for helping me put words to the message God put on my heart.

Lysa TerKeurst, you have been a God-given lifeline through this process! Thank you for your wisdom, timely words of encouragement, and for helping me breathe through moments of sheer panic and anxiety over what I had gotten myself into. Thank you for being with me through the roller coaster of emotions at each step of the journey.

Thank you, Beth Adams, for editing the book and forming it into something greater than I could have ever imagined. Although it was challenging at times, I'm so grateful that you stretched me to write the message God put on my heart. I'm forever grateful for the opportunity to partner with you on this project. Thank you for making the dream of publishing my first book a reality.

Thank you to the entire team at Worthy Publishing. It has been such a delight to work with you on this project. Thank you for believing in this message and for helping expand its reach.

Thank you to the focus412 team for your encouragement, support, and prayers throughout this process. It is an honor to serve the Lord and build the Church with you, Philip and Angela Engle, Bethany Garcia, Betsy Lonsberry, Christy Ray, Hannah Pereira, and Heidi Morgan. A huge thank you to the friends who have gone out of their way to support me in this process by sending encouraging notes and texts, praying for me and the book, reading drafts, and consistently checking in. I am grateful for you Enjoli, KJ, Mandy, the Carters, and the Coxs.

Psalm 92:13 says, "Those who are planted in the house of the Lord Shall flourish in the courts of our God" (NKJV). I am forever grateful to have been planted in two amazing churches over the course of the past couple decades: Faith Church in California, where I served for sixteen years, and more recently Church of the Highlands in Alabama. It has been a delight to be in community with two incredible spiritual families who have taught me more about Jesus.

Jesus, thank You for entrusting me with this project. I pray the message reflects Your heart and draws people to You. Thank You for walking with me through the seasons of my life. I'm so grateful for Your unending patience, unconditional love, mercy, and grace. Thank You for all You have taught me and brought me through over the past four decades. There is no other place I want to be than in Your presence.

ABOUT THE AUTHOR

Grace Wabuke Klein and her husband, Phil, lead focus412, a ministry that helps churches grow. Through this ministry, they have worked with some of the most impactful and influential churches across the country. Grace was born in Uganda during the tyrannical reign of Idi Amin, and her family fled to the United States and settled in Minnesota. Grace has a bachelor's degree in US history from the University of California, Berkeley, and earned a master's in intercultural studies from Fuller Theological Seminary. She was on the pastoral leadership team at Faith Church in West Covina, California. For more than fifteen years, she had the honor of empowering thousands in their leadership and spiritual growth. Grace and her husband have been married for over five years and reside in Birmingham, Alabama.